Absolutely Organized

A Mom's Guide to a No-Stress Schedule and Clutter-Free Home

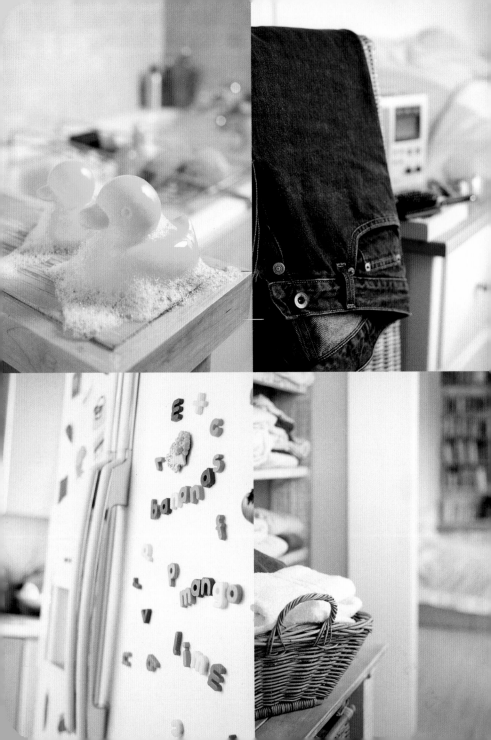

Absolutely Organized

A Mom's Guide to a No-Stress Schedule and Clutter-Free Home

DEBBIE LILLARD

NORTH LIGHT BOOKS
CINCINNATI, OHIO

Other fine North Light Books are available from your local bookstore, art supply store or direct from the publisher. Please visit www.fwbookstore.com.

12 11 10 09 08   5 4 3 2

Distributed in Canada by Fraser Direct
100 Armstrong Avenue
Georgetown, ON, Canada L7G 5S4
Tel: (905) 877-4411

Distributed in the U.K. and Europe by David & Charles
Brunel House, Newton Abbot, Devon, TQ12 4PU, England
Tel: (+44) 1626 323200, Fax: (+44) 1626 323319,
Email: postmaster@davidandcharles.co.uk

Distributed in Australia by Capricorn Link
P.O. Box 704, S. Windsor NSW, 2756 Australia
Tel: (02) 4577-3555

Library of Congress Cataloging in Publication Data
Lillard, Debbie, 1967-
  Absolutely organized : a mom's guide to a no-stress schedule and clutter-free home / by Debbie
Lillard.
    p. cm.
  Includes index.
  ISBN-13: 978-1-58180-955-8 (pbk. : alk. paper)
  ISBN-10: 1-58180-955-7 (pbk. : alk. paper)
  1. Mothers--Life skills guides. I. Title. II. Title: Mom's guide to a no-stress schedule and clutter-free
home.
HQ759.L54 2007
648--dc22
                              2007002796

Edited by Jacqueline Musser; Designed by Clare Finney; Production assistance by Jennifer Hoffman; Production coordinated by Greg Nock; All photos, unless otherwise noted, are by Alex Wilson/ Digital Vision/Getty Images; Photo on page 180 by Tim Grondin; Illustrations by Christine Erikson

ABOUT THE AUTHOR

Erinn Aloi, A fresh focus photography

Debbie Lillard is a professional organizer and the mother of three young children. After starting her own organizing business in 2003, Debbie appeared on four episodes of HGTV's *Mission: Organization*. She has been referenced as an organizational expert in articles for *The Philadelphia Inquirer* and on HGTV's Web site. She is a member of the National Association of Professional Organizers. Debbie has a BA in Communications from Marymount University, and worked as a technical writer in sales training for a major telecommunications company before becoming a "stay-at-home" mom.

DEDICATION

To my family

ACKNOWLEDGMENTS

I would like to acknowledge all the people who have helped me achieve this life-long dream of becoming an author. My heartfelt thanks goes out to the people who helped me get started in my professional organizing business, namely my friend Mary, who was my first client; the Havertown Moms Club, which was my focus group and the source of many ideas; Nancy Glass Productions who hired me for *Mission Organization*; and of course, Nana and Grams who were the best baby-sitters I could ask for!

Secondly, I want to thank those who helped me take my big idea and make it a reality including: Dave, the other Lillard author, who kept asking me, "When are you going to write that organizing book?"; Jamie and Jackie at North Light Books, who believed in my idea and guided me through the process; and my good friend Michele who helped me with editing and proofreading.

Lastly, I must thank my husband, my family and my close friends who have always given me the encouragement and support to do anything I set my mind to. I hope that this accomplishment of mine will inspire them, especially my children, to reach for their dreams wherever they may lead.

Introduction

In my experience as a professional organizer, I've noticed two things about the moms I've worked with: first, they need organizing help not because they are lazy, but because they are busy, and second, they are usually very hard on themselves. Let's face it, the job of a mother is multi-faceted. Maybe you're not the most organized mom on the block. But you may be the best cook, or the most fun to be with, or the one who gets involved in your child's school. Recognize your strengths along with your weaknesses. If you need help organizing, you've come to the right place.

There is no right or wrong way to organize. There is only what works and what doesn't work. I have noticed, however, that there are similar habits among people who are organized. I call these my "Absolutes of Organizing" because they are rules that you absolutely must follow if you are going to be an organized person. You will find my absolutes highlighted throughout the book and then listed on page 186 in the appendix.

If you enjoy your home and can feel relaxed there, if you pay your bills on time, rarely lose things, can get places on time and have what you need, then your system of organization is probably working. However if the opposite is true and you

> *There is no right or wrong way to organize. There is only what works and what doesn't work.*

feel stressed out at home, can't find anything, are always rushing and being late, and have numerous unfinished projects in your house, then it's time for a different approach.

If you feel like a mess, then congratulations! You've taken the first step toward improving your situation. The next step is to find your motivation. This is what will keep you going in the middle of a big project. Do you want to simplify your life so you can relax more? Do you want to arrange your home so you're not embarrassed to have guests over? Do you need to set up your paperwork so you can save money and time? Do you want to get rid of the excess in your life so others can benefit? These are all good reasons to get organized. Write down your motivation and look at it every day. Then read through this book from start to finish.

First, we will organize your time so you can take care of the day-to-day and still have time to accomplish some cleaning out projects. Then we will discuss how to organize your belongings category by category. In some cases you may need to gather it all up from various rooms just to see how much you have. Finally, we'll organize your home room by room. Make it a game and have fun. Be realistic with what you can save and toss. Above all, realize that organizing is like dieting. You can't do it fast and furious for two weeks and think you are done. You have to incorporate organizing into your daily life if you really want to change the way you are living. Your family is your support system, so include them in making decisions. They will have more interest in helping you keep things organized if they are part of the picture.

This is a book full of tips and hope. You will find a "place for everything" and when everything is in its place, life runs more smoothly.

Part I: Organize Your Time

PLAN YOUR WORK AND WORK YOUR PLAN. Mary Kay Ash, founder of one of the world's largest cosmetic companies, taught her directors to "plan their work and work their plan." I learned this as an Independent Beauty Consultant, one of the many part-time jobs I had as a young mom. All you need to accomplish something is to plan the work. The work might be decorating a house, packing for vacation, or starting your own business. Once you have a solid plan—a list of what needs to be done—you must work that plan. In other words,

just do it—and don't second-guess yourself. Many times I venture into a project and start doing things not in my plan. Then I get distracted and everything takes longer than anticipated. At some point I make myself refocus and go back to my list. If I stick to the plan, I usually accomplish my goal.

> *"He who every morning plans the transaction of the day and follows out that plan, carries a thread that will guide him through the maze of the most busy life. But where no plan is laid, where the disposal of time is surrendered merely to the chance of incidence, chaos will soon reign."*
>
> —VICTOR HUGO

1. The Housework Never Ends!

THE PROBLEM

Maybe you were an organized woman B.C. (Before Children). Many of us were. When you only have yourself to care for, things are pretty simple. Even if you weren't the most organized person, all you needed to get back on track was a Saturday morning cleaning frenzy. Now that you're a mom, your time is not your own. You are at the mercy of your children's schedules and their basic needs. Each day you must consider the household responsibilities, the family social schedule, the medical needs of the children and often your own work obligations. Get back on track? That could take months! It often seems impossible to handle. Does this sound like you?

You find yourself forgetting appointments

You're always running late

You run around but never feel like you accomplish anything

You can't find time to talk to or see your best friends

You have no time for yourself

You dream about things you'd like to do but never get around to
   doing them

The first thing you need to work on is your time management.

Time management boils down to two things: planning and finding balance.

THE STORY

I have worked with several mothers who do not work and do not have young children at home. So when I hear that their excuse for being unorganized is "I just don't have the time," I have to hold back my scream. They're last-minute shoppers for gifts and food for dinner, and they just can't get to their paperwork piles. They have projects that they have been meaning to get to but just can't. They are not lazy people. They are constantly moving and doing, but they never seem to accomplish an end result. The problem is that they don't have a schedule or a plan to achieve goals.

THE SOLUTION

I believe time management boils down to two things: planning and finding balance. A mom who plans her time carefully can achieve balance between:

- household chores and mothering
- being a mom and being a wife
- family time and personal time

This balance brings happiness and contentment to your life. Sounds ideal, I know, but it is possible. Think about when you feel your worst as a mom. Does it happen when you've only been doing one thing? If all you do is household chores, do you feel like a maid? If you work outside the home too much, do you feel like your mothering is lacking? And if you are always with your husband and children, do you feel like you've lost the individual woman you once were? If you are never alone with your husband do you lose the romantic feeling you had when you were dating or first married? Balance is the key and if you want it to happen, you have to plan it! Most things don't happen by accident.

Start the Day Off Right

The most important time management skill involves how you start your day. Think about what you need to do or would like to do each morning to get yourself off to a good start. It might be exercise, showering, walking or having a cup of tea or coffee, or it might be simply to sit in quiet to read or pray. Answer this question for yourself: "What do I wish I could do every morning before the rest of the family is up?" Then get up at least thirty minutes before your earliest riser and do it. Take care of yourself before you have to take care of everyone else for the day. Too many moms wake up, roll out of bed and start right in on taking care of the children, making breakfast and packing lunches. Before they know it, they have to drive someone to school and they haven't even brushed their teeth yet! It's worth getting up a little earlier to start each day on your own terms.

Another morning ritual is to make sure the bedrooms are tidy before you go downstairs for breakfast. This includes: making the bed, putting clothes away and picking up any stray items that need to go downstairs. As the children get older they can help with their own rooms.

Absolute of Organizing: Daily routines are a must.

Work When You Are at Your Best

When establishing your new organizing habits, consider your own energy levels and your schedule. Are you a night owl or an early bird? If you need to be out of the house early in the morning, it makes sense to accomplish as much as possible in the evening. You can tidy up, set the coffee maker, make the children's lunches and plan your next day after the children go to bed. Then you can relax and not worry about tomorrow. One mom I know has a great tip for making lunches ahead of time: When she buys lunch meat, she immediately divides it into sandwich-size portions and freezes them in little sandwich bags. Each night, she takes one portion out and puts it in the refrigerator. By morning it is thawed and ready to make a quick sandwich. This also saves money because it keeps the meat fresh and you never have to throw out slimy meat at the end of the week!

If you work in the evening, or simply have more energy in the morning, then kick up your feet at night and follow my suggestion of rising before the children. People sometimes ask me, "What should I do first in the morning to be organized?" I tell them there is no right or wrong way to organize your time. There is only what works and what doesn't. Everyone's family is on a different schedule with work, school and little ones' sleep habits. Determine your best energy time and plan your day around it.

Use a Daily Planner

Another important step in organizing your time is choosing a daily planner in a size that works well for you. It could be an electronic organizer or a paper one. I use a Franklin Planner that has a month-at-a-glance, daily pages with plenty of room for my list of things to do and a clean page for notes. I started using

Daily planners are a great way to keep track of your appointments, tasks and errands.

a planner like this when I was working at a large company. When I decided to be a stay-at-home mom, I thought I would never need that level of detail again since my days would be spent in domestic bliss. Taking my child to the park and making wonderful dinners for my family would be my focus. I could watch TV and play blocks

I think about how to group tasks together to be more efficient.

at the same time. Who needed a list of things to do for that? It didn't take me long to realize how wrong I was. A few years and a few kids later, I was making doctor's appointments right and left, signing up for kiddy activities, starting my own business, undertaking home decorating projects and doing all the usual household chores. How could I fit it all in? I quickly ordered the refills for my planner and began to write it all down. I also formed the habit of taking a few minutes every morning to make a list of things to do in my planner. Now it's as habitual as my morning coffee. I think about how to group tasks together to be more efficient. I usually do my errands in the morning and plan which store to go to first if there is more than one. My toddler naps in the afternoon, so that is when I can do important things at home such as computer work or phone calls.

Absolute of Organizing: Group like things (or tasks) together.

To kick off this habit, limit your list to the five most important things you must do each day. A longer list may be too overwhelming to achieve. This will also help you focus on priorities. The daily planning process takes about ten minutes. You can do it either first thing in the morning or right before you go to bed, whenever you can think clearly. If your list is longer than five items, I suggest using the FranklinCovey method of prioritization:

Items marked A = must get done today

Items marked B = should get done today

Items marked C = would be nice to get done today

Then number the tasks with 1-2-3, etc., within each category in the order they should be completed. Check your progress around lunch time and re-prioritize if necessary. At the end of the day, if something is not done, move it to tomorrow's list or to the next logical day that it could be done. If all five things get done before the end of the day, you can add some less important items to the list, or take the rest of the day off to do some fun things.

If you decide to use an electronic planner, the method is the same. Use the "calendar" to plug in appointments or places you have to be. Then use the "tasks" list to put in the things you have to do each day.

You can also create other lists in your planner such as "Books to read," or "Places to go when friends come to town"—any lists you can imagine that will help you remember things. Many people create lists, but if these lists are on little pieces of paper throughout the house, they get lost and there's no continuity from day to day.

With a planner you can refer back to what you did yesterday or last month. Many times I've used my planner as a reference guide. If I can't remember if I called someone or sent a thank you note, I check back in my planner to see if I did. If a bill comes in with a late fee, I check to see when I mailed it. All these things are recorded in my planner along with other vital information. This level of detail may not work for you right now. Remember there is no "right" or "wrong" way to organize. Start simply and decide how you can make a planner work for you.

Keep a Notebook Handy

If you write lists and reminders to yourself all over the house and can never seem to find the right one on the right day, try this trick. Put a notebook and pen wherever you do your best thinking. For some it's in the car, or in the bathroom, or in bed at night. Have a note pad handy so you can write down the little tidbits that pop into your head. Then transcribe them into your daily planner or electronic organizer. Once it's written down, you don't need to think about it anymore, and once it's in your planner, you know that it will get done.

Tracking Expenses With Your Planner

HAVE YOU EVER started the week with $100 and by Friday you're down to $5? Where did the money go? Cash has a way of slipping through our hands, doesn't it? My husband, who is an accountant, taught me a simple trick when we were first married. Write it down in your daily planner! For instance, today I started with $20 in my wallet. I spent $5 on food and $7 on greeting cards. I should have $8 left at the end of the day. Once you have captured this information for a year, you can use it along with your checkbook ledger and credit card statements to create a family budget. But even if you don't strictly budget, you will have a sense from day to day where your money is spent. If you are ever questioned by your spouse—where did that $100 go?—you'll have an exact answer. This is a step that takes minutes to do each day and will give you vital information in the long run.

Absolute of Organizing: Start with a good list.

A daily planner is your best planning tool to use at the beginning and end of every day. You will feel accomplished as you check things off your list. You may even find that by planning things out, you have more free time than before. In other words, you'll be looking for things to do! That's when you can balance your time with things you like to do or want to do.

OCTOBER

SUN	MON	TUES	WED	THURS	FRI	SAT
	1 mom works 6-8	2 dance 5	3 mom works 10-2	4 ortho 4	5 soccer 6	6 soccer 12
7	8 **kids off** COLUMBUS DAY	9 dance 5	10	11 mother's club 10-2	12 soccer 6	13 soccer 2
14 church picnic 12-3	15 mom works 9-11	16 dance 5	17 mom works 10-2 PTA 7	18	19 mom works 9-1 soccer 6	20 soccer 9 smith's 8
21	22 mom works 9-4	23 dance 5	24	25 mom works 9-4	26 soccer 6	27 soccer 10
28	29	30 dance 5	31 HALLOWEEN			

A family calendar can cut down on paper piles by storing important information from incoming mail.

Family Calendar

Another tool that will help you on a day-by-day basis is the family calendar. I don't know how any mom can live without one. Choose an attractive calendar to hang in a prominent place in your home where everyone can see it or add to it. The kitchen is the most likely location for most families. You don't have to have a huge block for each day, just an average size will do for writing where you have to be. Abbreviate as much as possible, especially for things that occur several times a month. If you really want to be detailed, you can use different colored pens for each member of the family.

The family calendar is also where you can transfer information from incoming mail such as invitations or flyers about special events. There's no need to save an invite from a child's party once you have RSVP'd and you have the address or party location registered in your daily planner. Simply write on the family calendar "Ryan's B-day 3-5" and throw out the invitation. This will save you piles of paper in the long run!

SCHEDULE THE WEEKLY CHORES

As moms, we know there are things that have to be done on a weekly basis for the family to function. Yes, I'm talking about those household chores like cleaning, food shopping, doing the laundry and taking out the trash. For these tasks, I take my example from days gone by.

I had already decided to limit my big chores to one per day when my way of thinking was confirmed by a tour guide at a colonial plantation near my house. I was on a class trip with my daughter and we were learning about how they lived in colonial times. "You moms today are crazy," the tour guide said. "You'll wash and clean every day and run to the market several times a week. Back in colonial times, they would do one chore per day and on Sunday they would rest." Ahhh, simpler times! I would like to rest on Sunday, wouldn't you? So here's what I do to simplify my weekly chores:

Cleaning

I clean the whole house on Mondays. Weekends are usually a messy time in my house so it's better to clean after the hubby and kids have gone back to work and school. It's also a great way to start off the week. If you have small children at home, I suggest cleaning while they watch a video or take naps. Toddlers have a way of slowing you down with their "help." Now that my youngest child is in preschool a few mornings a week, I clean while he's gone so I can spend time with him when he's home.

By cleaning I mean scrubbing bathrooms and floors, dusting, and vacuuming. When not interrupted, I can clean the whole house in two hours. That includes four

Cleaning thoroughly each week may seem like a lot to do, but I look at it this way: I clean for my family, I straighten up for company.

bathrooms, four bedrooms, a living room, dining room, kitchen and family room. Cleaning thoroughly each week may seem like a lot to do, but I see it as part of my overall job of keeping my family healthy. I look at it this way: I *clean* for my family, I *straighten up* for company. Cleaning every week has several other benefits:

- it forces you to keep clutter to a minimum
- you can see what needs to be repaired throughout the house
- you can find misplaced items as you clean
- if you miss a week for an emergency, it's okay.

Laundry

I wash all our clothes on Friday. Everyone has clean clothes for the weekend, when we dress up more than during the week. We usually have about six loads, so it's an all-day project, but it doesn't stop me from doing something fun with the kids that day. I sort the dirty laundry in my bedroom first thing in the morning. Then I put a load in before breakfast and continue to "swap the wash" between washer and dryer in between other things I do that day. I choose not to fold as I go but move the clean laundry bins to the family room. Then at the end of the day, or during the baby's nap time, I sit and fold as I watch TV. It's actually very relaxing. If you're someone who has a lot of ironing to do each week, you could fold as you go and iron in the evening. Or do the wash one day and the ironing the next. Friday night, my husband and I deliver each child's basket to his or her room and all but the three-year-old put their clothes away. If everyone in your family has at least seven pairs of underwear and socks, you can do this too! One bit of advice is to have a laundry bin in each person's room. One bin per household fills up very quickly! And if your family likes to deposit dirty laundry in the laundry room all week, then have separate bins set up for whites, dark colors and light colors.

Food Shopping

I usually shop for food after church on Sundays. Yes, I know I'm supposed to be resting but I like to have fresh food to start out the week. My husband is home then, so I can go by myself, which is a lot faster and less costly. I use a list that remains on our refrigerator at all times. I call it the perpetual food list. Anyone who finishes something or who has a request can write it on the list. I also think about what meals I will make for the week and check my recipes for ingredients we might not have. If planning meals is difficult for you, try to make a list of fourteen meals that your family will eat. If you can't think of that many, try ten at least. Post this list in the kitchen or keep it with your coupon caddy so you can consult it before you go food shopping. Try to rotate between five to seven meals this week and five to seven different ones next week. That will prevent your family from getting bored with the same old meals. Before I go shopping, I pull out the coupons I will use. Then I stick to the list.

If planning meals is difficult for you, try to make a list of fourteen meals that your family will eat. Post this list in the kitchen or keep it with your coupon caddy so you can consult it before you go food shopping.

That leaves four days of the week free from big chores! Some people think this schedule is inflexible and regimented. I say it is quite the opposite. With the type of work I do, my schedule is always changing. Typically, I don't schedule clients for Monday or Friday, but if I must, I can do my cleaning or laundry on one of the other days. Recently, I spent an entire Monday with my son, going to doctors and getting a cast put on. And guess what? I easily skipped cleaning that week because I knew I could get it done the following week. I didn't have to worry about buying food for dinner that night or doing the laundry because it was already planned out for the week. I could focus on the situation at hand, which was taking care of my son.

LOOK AHEAD MONTH BY MONTH

Once you have your daily activities under control, you can start to plan farther out. This is where the month-at-glance part of your planner and the family calendar come in handy. My planner has a list of goals at the beginning of each month

Use a monthly goals list for bigger projects that haven't been scheduled yet or projects that require multiple steps. Use your "month-at-a-glance" to schedule these projects or goals and your daily pages to write down smaller tasks.

that I find useful and easy to refer to. Ask yourself, "What do I want to accomplish this month?" Whether it's to get a haircut, paint a room, or plan a vacation, writing it down will help you remember and focus. Use the monthly goals list for bigger projects that haven't been scheduled yet or projects that require multiple steps. Use your "month-at-a-glance" to schedule these projects or goals and your daily pages to write down smaller tasks.

When you have household projects in mind, it's a good idea to plan them out by season. In the winter, you can work inside on painting and minor home improvements. In the spring, outdoor projects like planting, trimming hedges and fixing fences can get done before the summer vacation. Depending on where you live, early summer might be a good time for planting certain flowers or painting outside. The fall comes with its own chores, like putting away outdoor furniture and gathering leaves. Spread these seasonal projects across the "monthly goals" pages in your planner so you won't be overwhelmed when the time comes. You also can plan ahead for the cost of these projects. At the beginning of each month, write down exactly which day you are going to do these projects. I never like to talk about a project getting done "whenever we have time" because we all know when that is—never!

TIPS FOR WORKING MOMS

Moms working full time outside the home have a really tough job when it comes to organizing a family and house. If I were not at my house a good part of the day, things would suffer—I know that. Occasionally, moms who work full time outside the home will challenge my "daily routines" with questions like, "How can I dedicate a whole day to washing or cleaning when I'm at work?" The easy answer is this: hire someone to clean and give yourself a break! The more complex answer is to budget your time and delegate. Busy people may get more done, but everyone has a breaking point. You can't do it all. Let's look at the steps to getting the tasks of a working mom under control.

1. Make a list of daily, weekly and monthly chores/tasks.
2. Decide who does what. Involve your spouse and your children where possible, or look at what chores you can hire out.
3. Decide on what days the weekly and monthly chores will take place.

HOW OFTEN	CHORE	WHO?
Daily	Kitchen clean-up	All
	Make kids' lunches	Mom
	Cook dinner	Dad
	Go through mail	Mom and Dad
	Do homework with kids	Mom and Dad
	Pick up/straighten house	All
Weekly	Wash	All
	Food shop	Mom
	Clean	Dad
	Take out the trash	Mom and Dad
Monthly	Pay bills	Dad
	Miscellaneous shopping	Dad

Note: You may not be able to do all the wash in one night, but try to limit it to two nights. Some working moms also make cooking dinner a weekly event by putting together meals on Sunday and freezing them for the week.

BRAINSTORM ANNUAL VACATION PLANS

A great way to make sure you have a vacation plan is to start off the year with one. Our family typically does this the week between Christmas and New Year's. Decide how much money and time you can budget for vacations and then brainstorm with the whole family how you would like to spend it. Give the children parameters such as places within driving distance or one day trips. Get out a white board or a big piece of paper and write down everyone's ideas. Even if you can't do all the trips this year, you can save the ideas and re-evaluate them next year. Save the list in your planner of course!

CREATE ONE-ON-ONE TIME WITH YOUR CHILDREN

If you have more than one child, you know that one-on-one time doesn't always happen. From time to time, it's a good idea to plan "dates" with your children. Just a couple hours together doing something that they enjoy is all it takes. You could take your daughter ice skating, or your son to a make-your-own-pottery place. Or your husband could take one of them to a workshop at a home improvement store. In the hectic pace of life these days, this may sound ideal, but the special dates you have will be wonderful. The trick is to remember to keep making time for these activities. Many couples who have a son and a daughter tend to let Dad take the son and Mom take the daughter, but mixing it up can also be fun and beneficial for everyone in the family.

Absolute of Organizing: If you don't plan it, it won't happen!

SQUEEZE IN SOME TIME FOR YOU

Many moms I know complain that they never get time to themselves away from their children. It might seem selfish at first, but let's face it, we all need a break sometimes to be better mothers. Time away from your children will truly help you appreciate them and lower your stress level. It's just another means to balancing your life. First, ask yourself what you enjoy doing. Then think about how you can incorporate that activity into your life now. Maybe you could join a group that shares your talent, or take a class. Or plan a weekend doing what you enjoy. Time away from your children can be time spent with your husband or your girlfriends. I love going to the theater, so a few years ago, I bought subscription tickets to a local theater and rounded up a few girlfriends to go with me. It's not a lot of time or money but it is something we all enjoy. All it took was an idea, a few phone calls and some forward planning.

2. We're at the Baby's Beck and Call

THE PROBLEM

You have a new addition to your family, and now you are not getting a full night's sleep. You can't get anything done without the baby interrupting, and you have no time for yourself. Even your most basic needs take a back seat. Does this sound like your life? Take heart. It will get better. If you are a first time mom, know that millions of others have gone before you in this endeavor and survived. Everyone has a different approach to mothering, and you'll hear lots of advice. I will share with you my family's approach to the early years of having children and hope that you can adopt the main concept of my "schedule" and incorporate it into your life.

THE STORY

My mother raised six children and the only pediatrician I can remember seeing was also my mom's pediatrician when she was a child. When Mom found something that worked, she stuck with it. Her pediatrician had a plan for every baby. It included when to feed them, how much, when to put them to sleep and for how long. Some call it rigid, I call it genius.

THE SOLUTION

When my older sister and I started having our own children, my mother taught us to do the only thing she knew—follow the doctor's schedule. Since then, my sister and I typed it up, added editorial advice, and gave copies to hundreds of friends and cousins. I have friends who run into my mom at church and talk about how their baby is up all night, eating all the time, etc. She whips out a copy of the doctor's schedule and if they follow it, lives are transformed. I met another mother through my local mom's club who was raised by the same schedule. Also a patient of this doctor in Philadelphia, she hands out copies of the doctor's schedule to her friends and cousins and they all swear by it. Because I am not an expert on nutrition, I will not include the "what to feed them" portion of the plan beyond the first few months. Discuss your child's diet with your pediatrician. As an organizational expert, I feel this schedule can bring some sanity to a new mother's life, so I will focus on the baby time management.

SET THE SCHEDULE

When a baby is newborn, he basically needs to eat and sleep. You can use this plan whether you breast feed or give your baby formula. I went with breast feeding every four hours pretty early on with my children but most women feel comfortable with every three hours for the first two months. Then you can stretch it to every four hours as the baby gets older.

My mother used to say the goal is to have your baby up for two hours and then down for two. If you're feeding him or her every three hours, it's up for 1 ½ and down for 1 ½ hours. Try to follow this routine every day, remembering it takes three weeks to form a habit. Some days may be completely out of whack because of your life or the baby's mood. But having a routine that you can get back to is what gives a new mom sanity. If your baby wakes up at a time other than 6 AM, just start with that time and do the "up for two/down for two" routine. Sometimes you may need to wake your baby for a feeding to keep them on schedule the rest of the day. Some say this is crazy but it does pay off in the long run. The baby will take better naps and have more hearty feedings with this routine.

Manage the Baby's Routine

6 AM *Baby wakes up.* Feed her for 10 minutes on each breast or 4-5 ounces of formula. Keep her up for about 1 ½ to 2 hours.

Note: Keeping the baby awake at this point means having him or her around you, noise, and lights, in the baby carrier or swing, basically receiving some stimulation even though his or her eyes may be closed.

8 AM *Put baby back to sleep* in the crib, darken the room.

Note: This change in the environment to quiet and dark signals to the baby that it's time to sleep.

10 AM *Feeding time.* Wake baby about 30 minutes before if she is still sleeping. Feed baby as mentioned above and keep awake again for 1 ½ to 2 hours.

12 PM *Put baby back to sleep* in the crib and darken the room.

2 PM *Feeding Time.* Wake baby about 30 minutes before feeding time if she is still sleeping. Feed as mentioned above and keep awake again for 1 ½ to 2 hours. This is a great time (2–4 PM) to get fresh air in the nicer weather.

4 PM *Put baby back to sleep* in the crib; darken room.

6 PM *Feeding time.* Wake baby about 30 minutes before if she is still sleeping. Feed for 20 minutes or 4-5 ounces and keep baby awake until 8 PM.

8 PM *Put baby to bed* in the crib after a bath.

10 PM *Feeding time.* Wake baby for feeding and put back to bed immediately.

2 AM *Baby should wake up* in the middle of the night around 2 or 3 AM. Do not wake her: let her wake you for this one! And then put her right back to sleep after burping. Also, try to feed her in a quiet, darker environment at this feeding.

CREATE A ROUTINE FOR YOURSELF

As you can see there are three naps during the day for the baby. These times are strategic for you to take care of yourself and get things done. For example:

8–10 PM   *Eat breakfast*, shower and do something around the house.

12–2 PM   *Eat lunch*, make phone calls, pay bills, etc.

4–6 PM   *Prepare dinner* and rest!

The flip side of that is the time you have when the baby is awake. Then you can do things outside of the house with him or her:

10–12 PM   *Run errands*, visit with friends, go for a walk.

2–4 PM   *Play outside*, shop, pick up other kids from school.

I always felt the night time had some normalcy to it when the baby went to bed at 8 PM. Even though the baby would get up again around 10 or 11 PM, I felt like the day was winding down at this point, and my husband and I actually looked forward to that one-on-one time with the baby. If your husband is willing, I suggest letting him do the 10 PM feeding so you can get some rest. You can take the 2-3 AM shift.

My children were so accustomed to this schedule that at a summer party at a friend's house, my two-year-old son lay on a hammock and began sucking his thumb despite the people around and blaring music. I looked at my friend and said, "It must be 8 o'clock." I was exactly right.

Change as They Grow

Be sure to adapt the schedule to include notable benchmarks as your baby begins to grow. Not all babies follow this pattern but mothers who have followed this sleeping and feeding schedule agree that their babies begin to sleep through the night at about six to eight weeks. Be sure to adhere to your pediatrician's advice and follow common sense.

AGE	NOTABLE BENCHMARKS
6-8 Weeks	Baby should sleep through the night from 11 PM to 6 AM. No more 3 AM feedings!
5 Months	Baby should sleep through the night from 8 PM to 6 AM as long as she is getting enough to eat during the day (cereal, vegetables, fruit, etc.). You no longer should wake him or her for the 10 PM feeding. Generally speaking, once your doctor says to give the baby solid foods, the 6 AM feeding is just formula (or breast milk), 10 AM is breakfast, 2 PM is a big lunch, and 6 PM is formula, cereal and fruit.
9 Months	Baby becomes what I call a regular member of the family. In other words, she eats three meals a day at normal times and takes two naps a day for about 2 hours at a time. I used the 9-11 AM morning nap and 3-5 PM afternoon nap until my children were about 15 months old. Then I went to one afternoon nap a day until they absolutely wouldn't take it anymore, which was about four years old.

3. When Will They Learn...?

THE PROBLEM

All parents intend to teach their children well, but when it comes to time management and organizing, many of us fail the course. In an effort to give our kids a happy childhood, moms often end up doing too much for them and consequently turn them into non-functioning adults. The idea is to let go of certain things little by little, allowing the child to make some choices and take on some responsibilities. Sometimes the child will let you know when he or she wants to make decisions and sometimes you will have to let the child know.

THE STORY

Mom A has three children who are very independent. At age three each made it very clear that they would pick out their own clothes each day. So instead of arguing over what they would wear, Mom A decided to give the children parameters like: today is a pants and long-sleeved shirt day. The child could decide which pants and which shirt to wear. In this example, the clothing is appropriate for the weather and the child has the independence and decision-making power he or she desires.

In contrast, Mom B laid out her children's clothing each night so they only had to get dressed in the morning. This lasted until the children were about ten years old. One day the mother thought, "Why am I still picking out their clothing?" The answer is that she never passed on that responsibility, and the children never asked for it.

THE SOLUTION

Here are some guidelines about different responsibilities you can give to your children at various ages. Getting back to the idea of "time management," the more your children can do for themselves, the less you have to do for them! It's a win-win situation—you free up your time, and you teach the children to take care of themselves and eventually to help you around the house. Children who grow up like this are more independent and often develop better decision-making skills along the way. If you never had to clean your own room, make your own meal, earn your own money or plan how you would get your chores done, what kind of an adult would you be? Of course every child is different, so adapt these guides to suit your child's natural characteristics and abilities.

INCREASE CHILDREN'S RESPONSIBILITIES

The following chart offers a guideline of responsibilities you can give to children at different ages. Try some of these and test their limits. The key is to accept that at first (and maybe forever) they are not going to do it as well as you would. It's all part of letting go. Perfectionism will get you nowhere as a mom. And if you insist upon being perfect, you will end up with all the work back on your shoulders. Let them try, and teach them how to do it "as well as you." Then let them settle into their own ways of doing things. It's amazing how even the little ones will develop their own sense of style and personality.

Make Clean-up a Game

Here's a game you can play with your children: Right Room, Right Area, Right Container. This can be done in the morning for the bedroom area and at night for the downstairs or main areas of the house. It represents the three basic levels of organizing. I call it a "game" but the rules are very loose. Even a two-year-old can help clean up and get things to the right room. For instance, ask them to take all their toys to the toy room. That's the "right room." As the children get older they

AT AGE	TEACH THEM TO...
3-4	• Clear plates after meals. • Get dressed by themselves. • Match up socks when you're folding wash. • Put their toys away with a simple instruction such as "Put all the blocks in the red bin."
5-6	• Join in a family chore like picking up leaves or straightening up the house. • Follow a morning routine to get ready for school. (Write it down in on an index card and place it where the child can see it.) • Set the table. • Put their clean laundry away. • Straighten their rooms.
7-10	• Clean their own rooms. • Help serve meals. • Bathe or shower by themselves. • Decide which activities and sports they will join.

continued on next page

AT AGE	TEACH THEM TO...
11-13	• Take on certain weekly chores like taking out the trash, doing the dishes, folding the wash, mowing the lawn, etc. • Plan out how they will complete long term projects for school by setting interim deadlines on a calendar.
14–18	• Baby-sit younger siblings. • Make a meal for the family. • Have a part-time job and budget their money. • Make important decisions about college and their future.
18 & up	• Be an independent adult—at this point the "child" should be treated like a roommate with regard to sharing the household workload and contributing to the household budget.

can determine where the "right area" would be, such as getting the toys into the toy box or on a shelf. The next level of detail is to have all the pieces of a particular toy or game in the right container. If your children aren't old enough, then "right container" is your responsibility. At least you had help on the first two steps! Use this game as a quick way to tidy up before company comes over, and as an everyday task to keep things in order. If you are so exhausted at the end of a day that you can't imagine putting one more thing away, try to push yourself to at least get things to the right room. It will make things better in the morning. Also you can reverse the game as the children get older: Mom gets the items to the right room and the children put the items in the right area and container.

Use a Stair Basket to Save You Steps. As part of your game of getting things to the right room, I highly recommend a stair basket if you have stairs in your house. A stair basket is simply a temporary place to store items that are on the wrong floor and a vehicle for making your cleanup easier. The caution here is that many people fill the basket and forget about it for days. Then the basket becomes merely another junk drawer. Develop the habit of emptying it each night when you go upstairs and each morning when you come down, and make sure the children help you put the items away.

LIMIT ACTIVITIES

Another valuable time-management lesson we can teach our children is to limit their activities. In today's society children are extremely overbooked. It is a rare neighborhood where you can find children playing outside after school. Most are running here and there for sports, lessons, etc. Some have to cram in homework before they go

A stair basket will save you time and effort when tidying up. Just remember to empty the basket every day.

to their activities in the evening. Hence the popularity of the scheduled "play date." We have to plan our children's play time around their busy schedules.

Activities are great. They expand our children's minds, exercise their bodies, and teach them teamwork. However, doing too many activities can cause stress, leave little time for homework, and take away their freedom to use their imagination to figure out how to play on their own.

I recommend limiting activities to one sport per season and maybe one other organized activity like scouting, music lessons or community service. There's no magic number but you should consider the time commitment involved in each activity.

When children are young (ages four to six) is the time to experiment with different activities. They will probably want to try everything their friends are doing at that stage. As they get a little older (ages seven to eleven) they will discover what they are good at and what they enjoy. You can ask their opinion about what sports they like to play, what instrument they would like to play and what groups they would like to be a part of. As your children move from middle school to high school (ages twelve to eighteen) their options will change about sports and activities. You can help them make decisions by narrowing their choices and asking them to choose. You can also help by showing them on paper what their schedule will look like with all the extra-curricular activities plugged in. Children know what they want *now*; they aren't accustomed to thinking in long term. Sometimes you have to think for them and involve them in the decision. Limiting activities for your children also will have benefits for the whole family, such as:

1. You won't have to drive them somewhere every night of the week.
2. They will have ample time after school to do homework.
3. They will have free time to use their imagination and just play!
4. It will save you money.
5. They may remember this lesson as adults and not become stressed out and over-committed.

FINISH ONE THING BEFORE YOU START THE NEXT

In the age of Attention Deficit Disorder, finishing one thing before you start the next is so important that it's one of my Absolutes of Organizing. As parents we can be a good example and a teacher on this matter. I have developed the habit of saying, "I will be there as soon as I finish what I'm doing" whenever the kids yell "Mom!" from the other room or ask me to do something when I'm in the middle of something else. I let them know that I've heard them but I also indicate that what I'm doing is important.

I believe this gives the children a good example of limiting distractions, and it teaches patience. Also, if I'm playing with the children and they go on to

Work From Left to Right

ANOTHER TIP THAT CAN HELP you with anything from putting on make-up to making a recipe is to work from left to right whenever possible. Spread out your ingredients on your left, and as you use an item, move it to your right. When your left side is empty, you're done. This is a simple routine with big impact. Think about how many times you are interrupted by your children throughout the day. Have you ever stopped in the middle of a recipe, left the room to take care of a child then returned and thought, "Did I put the sugar in?" If it's on your left, the answer is no. Likewise, have you ever been in the middle of your beauty routine and thought, "Now, did I put on my deodorant yet?" Moving from left to right helps us stay on track when our lives are full of distraction.

something else, I ask, "Are you finished with this?" If the answer is yes, I suggest they put the toys or game away before we go on to something else.

This rule also applies to items that you are using like ketchup, toothpaste or a bottle of bubbles. How many times have you looked in the bathroom cabinet and seen three tubes of toothpaste all half full? What happened? Did you start a new one because the flavor was better? Or did the old one dry up? Whatever the case, finish the old one or throw it out before opening a new one. This prevents clutter and waste.

Absolute of Organizing: Finish one thing before you start another.

4. Are We Having Fun Yet?

THE PROBLEM

Certain times of the year are supposed to be joyous and magical for your family, like Christmas and vacations. But for us moms, the planning and wrapping and packing for these events can be so time-consuming and stressful that when the special day arrives, we just want to curl up in a ball and sleep!

THE STORY

Here's a tale of two Christmases. A mother of six frantically runs to the store at 5 PM on Christmas Eve. Her teenage children are baking cookies and trimming the tree. Frozen pizza is the meal for that night. As the children are dreaming of the wonderful toys that will appear tomorrow morning, Mom and Dad are up until 2 AM wrapping presents and putting toys together. The children awake at 6:30 AM ready to see what Santa has left. Mom and Dad beg them to stay in bed one more hour.

Another Christmas, Mom has done all her shopping online by December 6. The house and tree were decorated by December 17, when they had a little cocktail party for couples in the neighborhood. On Christmas Eve, the family has a nice lasagna dinner and they go to church at 7 PM for the candlelight service. After the children are in bed, Mom and Dad place the presents around the tree, put one toy together and have a glass of wine. They go to bed at 11 PM and awake at 6:30 AM with the children.

THE SOLUTION

My solution is to plan ahead, be efficient with preparation time, and keep it simple. Then you can enjoy yourself when that magical day arrives.

TAKE THE "BAH-HUMBUG" OUT OF YOUR CHRISTMAS SEASON

Our society makes such a big deal about the Christmas season that red and green decorations appear in stores before all the Halloween candy has been eaten. I've told myself many times that I'm not going to think or worry about Christmas until after Thanksgiving. But if you go shopping, you can't avoid it. So think about the holiday in a "planning ahead" way as opposed to a "buying frenzy" way. In planning any big event, you should start with a good list and a budget.

Create Christmas card labels. Right now, you probably have a good idea of who you like to send Christmas cards. If you are working from a handwritten address book that is wearing out, it's time to join the age of technology and put your Christmas card list on the computer. Find a way to create a sheet of mailing labels. If you don't have the skills to create one yourself, have a friend or one of your children create one for you. Name the file "Christmas Cards" or "Addresses" or something simple, and update it throughout the year. I usually print out this file on regular paper in late November. My husband and I look it over to see who we want to add or subtract, or if there are any addresses we need to get. I mark the changes on paper, key them into the file, and print out the labels. I use a decorative type font and clear mailing labels that can be purchased at any office supply store. When it comes time to send Christmas cards, we have an assembly line where I sign the card, someone stuffs the envelope and someone else puts the mailing label and stamp on. This can be done in one evening early in December.

Make two gift lists. An essential list for Christmas is the list of people you want to buy gifts for. This list should include family members, teachers or neighborhood helpers (like the baby-sitter or the bus driver), office Pollyannas, and charity donations. Put the list in your daily planner so you can add to it as you go about your normal day.

> *Remember, the more you buy, the more you have to organize.*

The second gift list I keep in my planner all year long is a list of gift ideas for my family members and close friends. Sometimes I see a book or a clever toy and think, "My nephews would like this." If I don't write it down, I'm at a loss for what to get them when it comes time to shop. Like the perpetual food list, it's a perpetual gift list which can be used for Christmas and birthday ideas.

Set a budget. Remember, the more you buy, the more you have to organize! So look at your list and set a reasonable limit for your family. Write down the budgeted amount next to each name, and when you buy the present, record the actual price. Keep in mind that younger children do not know the prices of things. If you're trying to keep it even among the children in your family, look at the number of presents instead of the cost. It's normal to spend more on the older children and less on the little ones. Don't feel bad, their time will come!

There are many sales around Christmas time, so if you buy a $25 sweater for $15 and your budget for that person was $25, don't feel like you have to spend $10 more. They are receiving a $25 present. Keep the difference (you might need it for someone else's gift) and move on to the other people on your list.

Once you decide your total budget, think about how you will pay for these items. Will you use one credit card for everything? Will you pay cash? Or will you do a combination of the two? Whatever the case, make a decision and stick to it. I also recommend saving all the Christmas receipts in one envelope in case someone needs to return something after the holidays.

Shop efficiently. In this age of technology you really can make your shopping easy if you want to. First, decide what type of shopper you are: do you like to take

One way to shop efficiently is to buy the same type of present for several people.

your time and be inspired as you browse, or do you know exactly what you want for each person and it's a matter of getting it? If you enjoy going out to the stores, start looking at the newspapers in November and keep ads from stores that you want to go to. Map out which stores are close together. If you want to spread out the shopping, plan to go to one or two stores each day. That way you won't feel rushed. Some people like to pick up Christmas gifts all year long, but if you do this you have to have a hiding place where you can store them and not forget about them!

If you are someone who doesn't buy until you know exactly what you want, I suggest shopping online whenever possible. You can shop at several stores in one hour if you do it that way! Another way to shop efficiently is to buy the same type of present for several people. For example, if you are buying gifts for four teachers, give them all the same thing.

Try to finish your shopping a few days before Christmas. It will give you time to wrap presents, prepare the holiday meal and enjoy the beauty of the season.

Decorations. One of the first things I do to get ready for Christmas is to pull out the decorations around the first weekend in December. I love to put the electric candles and wreaths in the windows so our house is decorated from the outside. Then I have the kids help me spread our inside decorations through-out the house. The last decorating we do is the Christmas tree, which usually happens one week before Christmas. We typically take it down one week after New Year's Day.

When packing away the decorations, I keep them separated by where they will go. All the little ornaments are carefully wrapped in smaller boxes inside a big plastic storage container. The outside wreaths, candles and extension cords are put into plastic garbage bags. The inside decorations fit into two other plastic storage bins. By separating them this way, I can take out one box at a time to do the decorating and leave the tree ornaments where they are until the tree is up in its stand. We decorate in stages, setting aside one day for each. Use your month-at-a-glance calendar to schedule these activities at the beginning of the month.

Decide where and when the festivities will take place. For many families, a source of the stress is where to go for the holiday meal. There are often two sides of the family to consider, and for some families, close friends or neighbors may want to celebrate with them. Decide where to go as early as possible. A standing tradition makes it much easier. When I was first married, my husband and I decided that we would alternate Thanksgiving, spending it with his family one year and mine the next. Christmas was more important to us, so we decided to spend Christmas Eve with his family and Christmas Day with mine. It's not always at the same place or the same time of day, but everyone in our family knows what to expect. This is especially important if you come from a family where guilt comes into play. First and foremost, you should consider how your immediate family wants to spend the holidays and how your children will feel about traveling on Christmas Day. Do what makes you happy and not necessarily what you think you "should" do.

Keep the meals simple. Where there are families and holidays, there is eating! A traditional Christmas meal of turkey or ham with all the trimmings looks wonderful in the magazines, but is it real-istic? And if you have two or more get-to-gethers over the holidays, can they all look picture perfect? Probably not. Sometimes it depends on what day of the week Christmas falls. If you are working until 4 or 5 PM on Christmas Eve, a big meal is not conve-nient. Have lasagna or pizza or sandwiches and save the big meal for Christmas Day. If you have a fancy Christmas Eve dinner,

If you are hosting the meal for a large group, there's nothing wrong with asking everyone to bring something.

serve cold cuts on Christmas Day. Like organizing, there's no right or wrong way to make the Christmas meal, there's only what works well for you. Keep this in mind before you set your expectations too high.

If you are hosting the meal for a large group, there's nothing wrong with asking everyone to bring something. You can take care of the main dish and other people can bring the wine, rolls, a vegetable dish and a couple desserts. If you're all going to Grandma's house, make sure you plan something for the children to do like a craft, a movie, or games. It will keep them from tearing apart Grandma's house and may give you some time to chat with the adults.

Follow these guidelines to plan ahead for your holiday season and your house will be decorated, presents will be wrapped, the meal will be easy to prepare and everyone will enjoy Christmas Day. Remember, it's the same time every year so there's no excuse for not being ready!

PACK UP YOUR FAMILY IN ONE WEEK

As a general rule, getting ready to go on vacation shouldn't take longer than the vacation itself. If you have implemented my tips for doing weekly household chores, you may have to switch things around a little the week before vacation. When you make your trip to the food store the week before vacation starts, include any special items that you will need to take with you. It's not an extra trip to the store, it's just a bigger order. When you wash clothes the week before vacation, pack everyone's clothes that night or the next day so they don't wear them before you leave.

A typical schedule the week before vacation may look like this:

Sunday – Check the weather for the place you are going so you can pack appropriate clothing. Cancel your newspaper and mail for the days you won't be home.

Monday – Clean the house. Print out your packing list.

Tuesday – Shop for sundries you will need.

Wednesday – Pack toys, books, music, etc.

Thursday – Wash and pack clothes.

Friday – Pack dry food. Drop off your pets if necessary.

Saturday – Pack cold food in cooler, and pack the car.

Be Adaptable to the Unexpected

I USUALLY PACK most of our food for the beach vacation we take every year. However, one year our refrigerator broke down and we had unexpected company the week before our vacation. Because it was such a stressful week, I cleared out the refrigerator into one cooler and packed whatever snacks we had in our cabinets. We ate dinner out the first night and I went food shopping the next morning when I was in a more relaxed state of mind. I don't usually like to go food shopping once my vacation has started, but in this case it was a necessity and it worked out just fine.

Make a packing list. Many families rent a house in the mountains or at the beach every year. If you take the same type of vacation every year, you can standardize your packing list so you don't have to start from scratch. Be general when you type up your list so you don't have to change it every year. For example, write "five shorts outfits, three pajamas" instead of "green shorts, tan T-shirt, blue pajamas, plaid boxers." I usually have my children, who are age six and older, pack their own clothes. I give them guidelines by telling them how many pajamas, short sets and bathing suits and let them decide which ones. I check the clothes before they go in the suitcase but they do most of the work. Then I give them each a bag to fill with toys, videos and books of their choosing. I give them the freedom to decide, but limit the space that all those items will take up.

For the food portion of the list, plan out dinners for the week and make sure you have some staples for lunch and breakfast. For the first night of vacation, it's

Use your list when packing up at the end of your vacation so you don't forget any odds and ends.

convenient to pack something pre-made so you can just pop it in the oven. For the last night of vacation, don't plan a meal. Just eat the leftovers from the week so you don't have to bring them back home. Depending on where you are staying and how close you'll be to a supermarket, you'll want to decide ahead of time whether to pack all the food or go shopping once you get there.

If you are taking a plane trip instead of driving, the packing is easier. Airlines limit what you can bring on board and you won't have to pack food. As you're making your list for this type of trip, think about what the children will need for the traveling portion and what they will want once they are at your destination. Plane trips can take longer than expected, so it's a good idea to bring some surprise toys or crafts with you. For my children's first plane trip, a friend suggested I bring Crayola Color Wonder coloring books and paints. These are finger paints and magic markers that look clear but turn colors on the special paper. They don't make a mess. My children had a ball with them.

Once your packing list is printed out, take it with you on vacation. As you think of things you need, add to the list. As you find things you packed but didn't need or use, cross them off. You can even use this list to pack up when vacation is over so you don't forget any odds and ends. When you get home, update the list on your computer so you're ready for next year.

Weather. I once heard someone say, "There is no such thing as bad weather, only inappropriate clothing." How true this is! You don't have to let bad weather spoil your vacation. You just have to have a Plan B. Use the Internet to check the weather for wherever you are headed so you at least have an idea about the temperature and precipitation. Pack umbrellas and waterproof jackets for everyone in the family even if it's supposed to be dry. Also consider the weather at home for your return trip. Have you ever seen someone at the airport in shorts when there's a snowstorm outside? That person came from a tropical climate and didn't think through what the weather would be like when he or she landed! You don't have to pack a parka, but at least dress in layers.

Travel Information. The Internet is also a great place to start when planning your trip. Look up the city and surrounding areas for things to do, or go to a Web site for your hotel to see what amenities they have. You can also make reservations for special excursions or restaurants through some Web sites. Investigate your vacation spot, print out what you need and take it with you on the trip. When you get home you can trash it because it's all still there on your computer.

While you're there. Have you ever had a vacation that was so packed with activities that you needed another vacation when you came home? Think about that before you plan your next vacation. You want everyone to have fun, but you also want to build in some relaxation. In my experience, the children are usually worn out by midweek of the first week of vacation. Whether it's the experience of an amusement park, going to a beach or visiting friends out of town, the change in schedules affects the children, so plan on it. Take one day and don't do anything extra. Sleep late, go to bed early, lie around and watch movies or whatever suits your family. Take a "Sunday" in the middle of your vacation week and recharge everyone's energy.

When children are infants, I'm a stickler for regular eating and sleeping schedules, but as they get older, you can be more flexible. If a toddler still takes a nap at home, you'll want to keep that routine on vacation or you will have one cranky toddler. Sometimes it's nice for you and your husband or the other adults with you to rotate "nap duty." One adult stays at the house with the sleeping toddler or baby. If you have other children, the person with nap duty really has the easier job! You could also move the nap a little bit later in the day, like from 3-5 PM while you're preparing dinner. Or if you are out at a theme

Take a "Sunday" in the middle of your vacation week and recharge everyone's energy.

park, plan to head home during nap time so the child can sleep in the car. Be flexible, but plan some nap time for the little ones and the whole family will appreciate it.

If you're at your vacation destination and the weather is horrible, make the best of it. Remember, you're still on vacation and away from the daily grind and normal routines, so take advantage of it. Play games like charades or cards, or do skits or sing songs. Bundle up and take a walk in the rain or the snow if you must. The children will take their lead from Mom and Dad, so remember to stay relaxed and positive and don't complain.

My husband and I once had a crazy trip to Paris where everything went wrong on the first day. We started playing a game called "It could be worse, we could be..." and we took turns finishing that sentence with outlandish situations. In no time at all we were laughing hysterically. When you're packing for vacation, remember to bring along your sense of humor!

Make Your Time Work for You

Now you have the tools you need to make your time work for you. An organized schedule is the first step to an organized home, family and life.

REMEMBER

- Assign weekly chores such as cleaning, grocery shopping, and laundry to specific days of the week.
- Use a planner to plan your days, weeks and months.
- Delegate or outsource chores so you do not have to do it all.
- Keep infants on a regular sleeping and feeding schedule.
- Teach your children responsibility by giving them tasks and chores as they mature.
- Limit your children's extra activities.
- Simplify your holiday season by creating mailing labels for cards, a gift list, and a budget.
- Keep a packing list for family vacations on your computer and update it each year. Let the children help you pack before your vacation.
- Plan downtime in the middle of your vacation week.

After following these tips you will find you have more time in your schedule to spend with your children, your friends and your husband. If you still need to organize the stuff in your house, read on! We'll discuss how to handle what tends to accumulate over the years.

Part II: Organize Your Belongings

ADMINISTER C.P.R. There's a bumper sticker that reads, "The one who dies with the most stuff wins!" I disagree. The one with the most stuff probably doesn't even know what she has. She probably doesn't treasure it or use it. In some cases she can't even find what she really wants in all that clutter!

If you want to rid your home of clutter, you must pare down your belongings to the most essential items. I call my organizing method "C.P.R.", which stands for: Categorize, Purge and

Rearrange. You start by putting like things together (Categorize). Then you eliminate excess by trashing or donating whatever you don't use, need, or like (Purge). Then you put the items back in a logical place (Rearrange). Think of it as breathing new life into your possessions!

"Out of clutter, find simplicity; from discord, find harmony. In the middle of difficulty lies opportunity."

—ALBERT EINSTEIN

5. The Paper Pile Keeps Growing

THE PROBLEM

Your house is overrun by paper. It covers every available tabletop in every room and it keeps coming in. When you need to find something important, it takes an hour. Your method of straightening up the papers involves shoving everything into a plastic bag and tucking it away when you have guests. Sometimes you'll go back to these bags and pull out what you need. Sometimes these bags will be forgotten for years.

THE STORY

One of my clients has a lovely home complete with two home offices: one for herself and one for her husband. However, the dining room table, the kitchen table and the kitchen counters are always covered with papers. So for those of you who are thinking, "I just don't have enough room for all this paper," I say it's not always lack of space that is the problem. It's often the fact that papers are not being dealt with in a timely fashion. As Barbara Hemphill says in *Taming the Paper Tiger*, "Paper clutter is postponed decisions. Paper management is decision-making."

THE SOLUTION

First let's deal with the backlog of papers in your house. Let's make those decisions you've been postponing, and then I will give you some suggestions for maintaining a paperless, or a "less paper," environment going forward.

DIG OUT FROM YOUR BACKLOG OF PAPERS

Bring it all in. Bring all your papers to a location where you can go through them. If your designated office is messy right now, take the papers to the cleanest room of your house. It will help you to think clearly as you decide what to keep. Getting all of one category in one place gives me a feeling of control. I think, *Okay, this is all of it. Now I just have to deal with it.* Then I start my C.P.R. process (Categorize, Purge and Rearrange). For some people though, the thought of all that paper in one place is overwhelming. If you see it, you might need CPR! So, if you cannot physically manage all of your papers at once, clear one room at a time. If one room is still too much, sort one box at a time, but still take it to a clear room.

Categorize old paperwork. If your backlog of papers is older than a year, there are probably just a few categories to sort them into: tax files, memorabilia, and important documents. Get three cardboard boxes and label them with these categories.

Tax files should go back seven years if you want to be conservative. Most accountants will say you are safe from audit after three years.

Memorabilia is always a sketchy area but make sure when you save something it's not "just because." Ask yourself, *Am I saving this to put in a scrapbook? Do I get pleasure from looking at it? Will I look at it again?* If you answer no to all of these questions, throw it out and move on. Remember your goal is to rid your life of old papers and clutter!

Remember your goal is to rid your life of old papers and clutter!

Important documents would be birth certificates, a marriage license, papers regarding the purchase of your home or vehicle—any large purchase that you currently own.

Purge what you don't need. Anything that doesn't fall into one of these categories and cannot be filed in an existing file cabinet must be trash. Keep a shredder and trash bag handy to destroy any trash containing personal information. Shredding is a task you can delegate to another member of the family or you can do it yourself while you're watching TV.

Decide where old papers will be kept. Important papers can be kept in a safe deposit box or a fireproof safe that you will keep in your house. Decide with your spouse where it will be located and where the key will be kept.

Memorabilia papers can be kept in a scrapbook or a manila envelope inside a bigger "memory" box. If you've got years of these papers, you can separate by people or era.

Tax files can be stored in manila envelopes marked with the year. The last seven years of envelopes can be placed inside a plastic storage box. Decide where these will be stored. Possible options are the basement, the attic or a closet in your office. Most likely you will only need to access this box once a year when you put the new year in and take the oldest year out.

Memorabilia papers can be kept in a scrapbook or a manila envelope inside a bigger "memory" box (see chapter seven for ideas). If you've got years of these papers and don't know how to put them in any logical order for scrapbooking, you can separate by people or era. If you have several children and have clippings that pertain to each, make a pile for each child. Or if you have general papers that you want to keep, put them in order by the era of your life. Some might be from grade school and high school, others from college, and others from your early years of marriage. Only you know the best way to break it down, but don't get overwhelmed by the process. It doesn't have to be perfectly chronological to make an interesting and enjoyable scrapbook or memory box. Just remember to keep like things together.

Absolute of Organizing: Keep like things together.

GATHER AND PURGE MORE CURRENT PAPERS

Once again, gather all your current papers together. These might be the ones on the coffee table, the kitchen table, the mail table or the top of your desk. Most likely these will be from the last twelve months or so. Now get three boxes and label them: TO DO, TO READ, and TO FILE. Take each paper and decide whether you need to DO something with it, READ it, or FILE it. This is how you categorize in a big way. Any of the papers you come across that do not need to be read, worked with or filed must be trash. So, have a large trash bag and a shredder handy.

Once you have sorted every piece of paper in your house you will need to deal with one box at a time.

Absolute of Organizing: Organize from big to small.

A desk or work area is a good place to keep your TO DO file. Make sure this file has a permanent home.

CATEGORY	EXAMPLE
To read	• Newsletters • Magazines • Catalogs • Personal letters • School flyers
To do	• Bills to pay • Invitations to respond to • Address changes • Requests from school that require a response • Bank statements to be balanced • Projects that you are working on right now
To file	• Credit card statements (separated from bill stubs) • Bank statements that have been balanced • Catalogs that you like to keep on hand • Receipts for charitable contributions • Statements from financial investments • Statements from utility bills • School reference information

TO DO box

- Add these items to your TO DO list in your planner.
- Prioritize when to accomplish the tasks. Urgent items should go on the list for today or tomorrow; something you'd like to get done this month goes on your monthly goal list; a goal that is not time-sensitive belongs in your planner for a future month.

Organizing Your TO DO File

IF YOU ARE CREATING THIS TO DO FILE for the first time, it might seem overwhelming. You may want to divide it into sub-categories and tackle one at a time. However, once you make it a habit to address these things every day, the pile will dwindle quickly! At first it's a project, then it becomes a daily routine. A typical daily TO DO file might contain something like this: two phone calls, one invite to decide on, four bills, two school forms to fill out and one on-going project.

- Whenever possible, write down the pertinent information and discard the paper! If you must keep that paper, put it in the back pocket of your planner or in the file marked TO DO.

- Decide where your TO DO file will reside. Keep it in the same place every day. A logical place is on top of your desk or wherever you sit to make phone calls, pay the bills, etc.

- Create an action file for projects in progress, such as school functions, planning a party for your family, or investigating pre-schools. An action file is simply a file folder to hold all the relative papers that go along with that project. It can be left out on your desk or in your "in" bin because you are using it daily. Once the project is complete, however, weed out the unnecessary information and file away anything you will need for future reference. Then add that file to your file cabinet.

- When it comes to updating addresses and phone numbers, it is easiest to keep them in a computer file. Then you can easily update changes as you receive them. There are several types of electronic address books, or you can create a Word document set up for mailing labels. This makes sending holiday cards and invitations easy. If you have a traditional address/phone book, always write in pencil so it's easy to change.

- You might want to separate bills to pay out of your general TO DO box so they don't get forgotten. One suggestion is to put them in due-date order on top of your desk in a napkin holder or letter holder. If you don't have many paper bills, you could tuck them in your planner's back pocket.

TO READ box

- Simply put it in a place where you like to sit and read.
- If you want to force yourself to go through the box, put it on your bed!
- Carve out a little time each day to read. Even ten to fifteen minutes a day helps keep this pile down.
- Once you have read each piece, discard it or file it.
- Occasionally what you read may become a TO DO, in which case you should write it in your planner and toss the paper. Or put it in your planner pocket only if it has important information on it that can not be found elsewhere.
- If your TO READ pile gets too large or too outdated, it's time to let it go! Discard it and be assured there's more on the way.
- A great time to purge a large TO READ pile is while traveling by plane, train or riding in a car. Take a stack with you and vow not to bring it home!

TO FILE box

- This may be the largest pile, especially if you don't currently have a filing system.
- If you have current files, go through them first and purge what you don't need before you put any new papers in.

Be realistic. Only keep or create a file if you will refer back to it.

Start by sorting all papers into major categories such as:

- Financial
- Life Insurance
- Home
- Medical
- Educational
- Legal
- Car
- Charitable Contributions

As you sort, you may find certain categories are larger than others. If a file is too full, you might want to break it down into more specific sub-categories such as:

- bank accounts
- report cards
- kids' activities
- credit cards
- medical insurance
- contractors
- medical reports
- utility bills
- home owner's insurance
- investments
- home improvement receipts
- warranties and instructions
- car insurance
- school information
- car maintenance receipts

Decide where your files will be kept. If you have a desk with file drawers, use it for the most-used files. Reference files can be stored in a file cabinet that is either in your home office, a designated storage area, or in a closet. For school information that you will refer to throughout the year, have a folder for each child. Most importantly, be realistic. Only keep or create a file if you will refer back to it.

Absolute of Organizing: Only keep what you use.

If you really want to be organized, put each major category of files in different colored hanging folders. Group like files together before you place them in your file cabinet.

MANAGE YOUR BUSINESS PAPERWORK

With so many network marketing companies and "home show" products, many moms run their own part-time business. If you are an independent consultant for a large company, the company may provide training about how to keep your books. Having done independent consulting myself, I will share some general guidelines for keeping this type of paperwork and bookkeeping under control.

Mileage Log: Keep a mileage log in your car for recording business miles. The log should include: date, starting mileage (from the odometer), ending mileage, total miles traveled and place or reason for the drive. At the end of the year, simply rip out these pages and total up the miles. Check with your accountant about the current mileage allowance you can claim on taxes.

Credit Card: Have a separate credit card for business expenses. Use it for things like office supplies, periodicals pertaining to your business, raw materials, and services such as Web site costs or cell phone charges. When the statement comes each month, file it in a "Business Expenses" file. Compile these at the end of the year for taxes.

Checking Account: Have a separate checking account for your business. Deposit your pay into this account and whenever possible write checks for your business expenses from this account. It will be easy to keep track of how much you are actually making at your part-time job! Again, your bank statements can get filed in "Business Expenses" so they can easily be compiled at the end of the year for taxes.

Contact Information: Contacts or leads can be kept in several different ways. The key is to consolidate names and contact information from business cards and little pieces of paper that you may accumulate. For many network-marketing businesses, following up is key. Possibilities for keeping your business contacts information include:

- A file box divided into categories like: new leads, call-backs, clients/customers
- An Excel spreadsheet
- A simple copybook

Cut Down on Junk Mail

ANOTHER WAY TO CUT DOWN ON YOUR PAPER FLOW is to remove your name from marketing lists. Each time you open a credit card or make a purchase via mail order or online, your name and address go on a marketing list. It's a good idea to contact the following agencies every five years to "clear the slate" and cut down on the sales offers you will receive by mail, phone or e-mail.

For credit card offers: Call 1-888-567-8688 to take your name off the credit information lists compiled by Equifax, TransUnion, Experian and Innovis.

For junk mail: Send a postcard with your name, address and the phrase "activate the preference service" to the following service: Mail Preference Service, Direct Marketing Association, P.O. Box 643, Carmel, NY 15012-0643. This will stop mail from all member organizations you have not specifically ordered products from in the last five years.

For general telemarketing calls: Call 1-888-382-1222 from all your phone lines or visit www.donotcall.gov online to be put on the National Do Not Call Registry set up by the Federal Trade Commission.

- Your e-mail program's address book
- A more sophisticated "contact" software program like ACT, GoldMine, Contact Manager Pro, Now Up-to-Date and FileMaker Pro, just to name a few
- Your "Contacts" list on your hand-held organizer

MAINTAIN YOUR PAPER SYSTEM EVERY DAY

Now that you have a place for all your papers, you need a plan to maintain your paper flow. Here are some daily habits to help keep the paper under control.

Mail: Deal with your mail every day. It requires making quick decisions but hopefully only a few each day. Sort into the same four categories mentioned before: TRASH, TO DO, TO READ, TO FILE. Take bills out of their envelopes, discard the excess paper, put the bill stub and return envelope in your TO DO or "bills to be paid" area, and the statement in your TO FILE area. Immediately trash junk mail, sales circulars that you're not interested in, and credit card offers—unless you are in the market for one of these products or services right now.

Children's Papers: Deal with your children's papers every day. Look at their schoolwork and ask them if they want to keep anything. If they do, each child should have a drawer in his or her desk or a box in his or her bedroom for schoolwork. Artwork can be displayed on the refrigerator, a bulletin board in the

Continued on page 74

A jute bin is an attractive way to store catalogs and newspapers.

How Long to Keep Statements

- **Utilities** – There's no need to keep these once the bill is paid, unless you want to compare year-to-year expenses. If so, two years is plenty.

- **Mortgage** – Save the last statement of the year if it has the "total interest paid" and "real estate taxes paid," which you may need for filing your taxes. Once it is paid off, keep the discharge statement as long as you own the property and six years after the sale.

- **Pay stubs** – Keep these for one year and check them against your W-2, then you may discard them and keep the W-2.

- **Car** – Save the sales contract and repair receipts for the life of the car.

- **Bank statements** – Keep for one year. Always balance your account on a monthly basis. If statements contain tax-deductible expenses, keep them with the tax information for that year.

- **Credit card statements** – If you use these for budgeting purposes, or if you will refer back to them, keep for one year. You may need to save the last statement of the year if you can claim the interest paid on your taxes.

- **Financial investments** – For tax purposes you will need to have proof of how much you paid for a stock and what you sold it for. Keep the purchase record as long as you own the stock and the sale record as backup information with your tax files for the year it was sold. If you have several dividends paid throughout a year, hold onto each until the investment company sends you an annual dividend statement. When in doubt, check with your accountant about what you need to keep.

- *Tax returns* – Keep a copy with all your backup information for seven years. Each year add one and discard the oldest one.

- *Medical bills* – Keep for the year if you itemize these on your tax return.

- *Medical reports/diagnosis* – Keep forever. As your children grow up and move out of the house, you can pass their medical file on to them.

- *Car/Health/Life/Homeowners insurance* – Keep current policies and claim information. In case of a claim against you, keep any previous homeowner and car insurance policies as long as the statute of limitations in your state.

- *Bill of purchase for property* – Keep for as long as you own the property.

- *Bill of sale for property* – Keep with tax information for the year in which it was sold.

Remember that most of these monthly and quarterly statements can now be electronically accessed. If you don't have a specific statement and you need it, you can usually contact that company to retrieve it.

playroom, or in a frame. The plastic box frames from art stores are great—they allow for easy updating. Throw out anything they don't want and you don't love. Read school flyers and treat them like any other mail. At the end of the school year, go through the box or drawer with your child. Anything you decide to keep will go into their memory box. Like your tax files, you can put papers in a manila envelope, and mark the grade or year.

Catalogs and Newspapers: Catalogs and newspapers tend to hang around the house for a while. I recommend having a specific, yet attractive place for each. Options include magazine racks, large baskets, leather carrying bins or some other decorative containers. Once the bin is full, however, it's time to weed out and recycle.

Sales Circulars: It's amazing how many of these we receive each week. I typically put these in the recycle bin immediately and here's why: They are designed to entice you to buy something you don't need! With my grocery list and other shopping lists that I keep in my planner, I know what I need to buy. Also, most grocery stores now have "clipless coupons." If you have a shopper's card for that store, you'll get the sale price anyway. However, with every rule there is an exception. If you are in the market for a gift or some clothing or household item and you want to find the best price for it, by all means look through the sales circulars, find the right store, cut out the coupon or ad that applies and place it in your TO DO file. You may even want to create a special envelope or folder to take with you when you are shopping.

When you return home from running errands, take five minutes to sort out your receipts from the day.

Receipts: While you're out running errands you will usually accumulate receipts. Take five minutes when you return home to sort them out. People often ask me, "How long do I need to keep certain receipts or bill statements?" Everyone's situation is different but I have some general guidelines that you can use:

- Receipts for cash expenses should be written down in your daily planner. Or if you keep your expenses on a computer system like Quicken, save the receipt in a small box or basket to record monthly.

- Credit card receipts should go in the file for that card and be stapled to the statement once it arrives.

- Check/debit card/ATM receipts should be entered into your check log each day. You can save the receipt in the back of your check log or in a file until the monthly statement arrives. Once you balance your account, you can shred those receipts.

- Receipts for gifts should either be kept with the gift or put in an envelope marked accordingly. Discard after you know it will not be returned.

- Receipts for major purchases should be kept stapled to the warranty or instruction book, in case of return.

6. So Many Photos—No Albums

THE PROBLEM

You have adorable, young children and you want to remember every precious moment of their lives—so now you are taking tons of pictures. But where do you put these photos? And when do you have time to organize them? Many of the mothers I speak with mention photographs as an area that they just cannot keep up with. If you are like them, maybe you are aiming for something too intricate and are ignoring simple solutions you can put in place right now to get your photos under control.

THE STORY

I once heard this tale at a Creative Memories scrapbooking demonstration: There was a family that cleaned out the parents' attic and fought over who would take the boxes of crumbled up and yellowed photos. No one wanted them!

Another family also cleaned out the parents' attic. This mother meticulously put pictures in an album and wrote notes next to each one. This family also fought over who would take the old photo albums—they all wanted to take them!

THE SOLUTION

If you want to enjoy your photographs, you have to do something with them! Leaving them in their original envelopes is not an option. Every picture tells a story so make your story a beautiful one by putting pictures in a place where you and your family will enjoy them.

DECIDE HOW TO ORGANIZE

All organizing starts with a decision. In this case, decide how you want to keep your photos or how you like to look at them.

Slip-in photo albums. These albums are the easiest to maintain and therefore are a good starting point for people who have photos in big boxes or in the original drug store bag they came home in. These are simply photo albums with plastic sleeves that you slip your photos into. Many come in a binder format so it's easy to move pages around or add pages. Some also come with a "notes" area so you can write interesting facts about each picture. You can put your photos in these first, and then pull out special shots as needed to put in frames or add to children's scrapbooks.

Slip-in photo albums are a quick and easy way to organize photos.

Corkboard wall. I have a good friend who loves to look at her pictures every day, so she put up corkboard on a wall in her kitchen from floor to ceiling and pinned her favorite pictures there. This is a great place to display holiday picture cards of family and friends. If you fill this area up quick, you'll have to remember to update it seasonally.

Collages. If you find that a lot of your pictures are not centered or close enough to the subject, you can cut out only the important people and important sites from a particular occasion and put them in a collage. It doesn't have to be fancy. Use a glue stick and glue them to the paper that comes with the frame. If you have a large blank wall in a family room, you can hang collages as you make them. Each frame will represent a different time or event in your life. They are fun to look at and they save a lot of space.

Photo boxes. Many stores carry these decorative boxes now. If you choose to use them, decide how you want to keep them: all family pictures chronologically or separated by each child? Make sure you label each box accordingly. Some of these boxes are so pretty you can leave them out on a bookshelf for easy access. I recommend putting the pictures in order and using cards to label and separate like you would a recipe file.

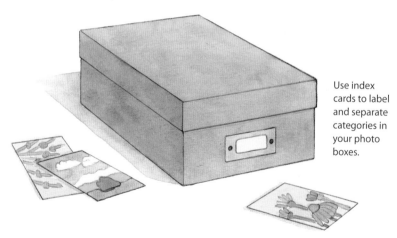

Use index cards to label and separate categories in your photo boxes.

Scrapbooks. This has become a favorite pastime for many mothers. The end result is beautiful and meaningful, especially when you "journal" or write little stories about what was happening during a particular event. The downside is that scrapbooks take a lot of time and creativity to put together, and it is a big project—not an everyday process. Even if you are great about keeping up with scrapbooks for your family, you need a staging area for the photos and memorabilia that will go into the scrapbooks. For this, I suggest simple household items like manila envelopes, plastic bins or shoeboxes. If your child collects pictures and pamphlets throughout the school year, drop them in the envelope or box and use the summertime to work on his or her scrapbook together. One of the best times for scrapbooking is a rainy summer day. I've even brought our scrapbook materials on vacation. When children are out of their normal environment, they look for different things to do, and scrapbooking can be a fun and creative outlet for them. Give yourself the whole summer. Take your time, create your scrapbook, and have an empty box ready to fill in September.

On your computer. If you have a digital camera, set up files of pictures on your computer. Here are some tips for organizing and using your digital photos:

- Give your files simple names. If you upload pictures from your camera once a month, name the file with the month and year (MAY08). If you upload less frequently, name the files by season and year (WINTER08). Or name them more specifically by event (VACATION08).
- Create digital photo albums on Web sites that you use for developing. This stores photos remotely and protects against a hard drive crash on your computer. The albums also store the photos in chronological order.
- Save your photos on a CD-R or DVD disk, which also protects them from anything that might happen to your computer. CD-Rs or DVDs take up a lot less physical space than photo albums but the photos are not as accessible to look at.
- E-mail digital copies of your pictures to family and friends rather than mailing them prints.
- Create a unique "slide show" screensaver on your computer with your personal pictures, and update it frequently.

START YOUR SYSTEM TODAY

Once you have decided how you want to store or display your photos, buy the items needed to carry out your plan and start with current photos. Purchase your storage boxes or photo album or corkboard now, and then you'll have a process for storing all the pictures you develop from now on. If you only develop between thirty and fifty pictures at a time, it should take you about ten to fifteen minutes to put them in an album or to hang them. If you typically get double prints, divide them up right away and put them in envelopes for the people you give them to. These envelopes can go right in your TO DO file. Once that process is in place, you can then address the old photos that are sitting around your house.

Gather Your Backlog of Photos

To begin organizing old photographs, I recommend you gather them all in one place. If you have an area where you can spread them out, or at least store a box of photos until your project is done, then move them into that area.

Categorize and Purge. Use the C.P.R. process (Categorize, Purge and Rearrange) and start categorizing the photos. There is no right or wrong way to do this. Group them by child, or time of year, or era. As you sort through, purge any pictures that are ruined or dark or blurry. Only keep the good ones!

Absolute of Organizing: Keep only what you use.

Arrange or Rearrange your photos. Finally, it's time to get your photographs where you want them. If you created a pile of photos for framing, start framing! If you decided you want them in an album, take a stack and start putting them in albums. Your children or your husband can help when you're all watching TV. If you want to make it really fun, give each child a stack of photos and a page or an album and see who can get their pictures in first.

If you want your photos accessible to the whole family and visitors, keep them on the bottom shelf of a bookshelf or console table in your family room or living room. I usually have six big albums on my bookshelf at all times. I often refer to them when I'm talking to my children about a trip we took, or someone they don't see too often. They really get a kick out of it. As the albums get older and more "beat up," I tuck them away in my memory box. "What's a 'memory box' and how do I get one?" you might ask. Read on to find out the answer!

7. I Keep Everything, but Treasure Nothing

THE PROBLEM

The first problem I often see when dealing with memorabilia is simply identifying exactly what in your house is "memorabilia." This may be new terminology for you. Ask yourself, "Why am I saving this?" If your answer is, "just because my kids did it" or "it brings back good memories," then that is MEMORABILIA. As mothers, we want to save every precious art project and little card or note that our children have written, but that's just not practical.

THE STORY

Before I had my first child, I went through a serious "nesting" time. One of the best things I did was to go through my "memory box." It was a steamer trunk that I took with me to college, then used as a night table in my apartment when I was single. It had slowly become the place where I kept all those little knick-knacks that you don't know what to do with but you don't want to throw away. It also held old letters that my husband had sent me while we were dating. I sat on the bed and read letters, leafed through my college and high school yearbooks, and looked at old photo albums. I picked up buttons and books of matches that

I had saved from special events, and looked at trophies that had once lined a shelf in my childhood bedroom. It was like I had found my own personal treasure box. I laughed, I cried, and I threw away what was stupid. But the emotions and memories it brought back were wonderful and in a way, it prepared me for the new stage of life ahead. I thought to myself, *Everyone should have a treasure box like this.* Years of memories were in one box and I knew where it was if I ever wanted to reminisce again.

THE SOLUTION

You must gather your memorabilia in one place to see the magnitude of your problem, if there is one. For some, this might be an overwhelming thought. I suggest tackling the accumulation of memories in the same way we tackled the overload of paperwork.

TREAT IT LIKE A SCAVENGER HUNT

Go from room to room in your house looking for things that you're hanging on to just because they remind you of a happy time. Once you've found your memorabilia, gather it into one room. If you can't physically fit everything in one room or on one table, start with one room at a time. You may have baby keepsakes for each child in their individual rooms. It makes sense to go through their items one room at a time. You may have the most memorabilia saved, and it may be stored in several places (your closet, the family room, the attic) in several containers. If this is the case, you may need to sort one box at a time.

Make a project plan. Decide how much time you will need to go through your memorabilia based on the amount of items you have collected. If you are doing one room, a two- or three-hour chunk of time in the evening may be enough. If you have several dozen boxes filled with memorabilia and you want to do it all at once, you're looking at a full day project. You need time to go through everything and purge what you don't want and group it into smaller categories. Once you know how much time it will take, put it on your calendar and TO DO list. You may need to ask your husband or a friend to help.

Begin to purge. Using my C.P.R. method, we have already "categorized" in the broad sense of the word, so now it's time to "purge." Purging memories is hard for many people but the process can be emotional in a good way, too. When was the last time you looked at your high school yearbook? Or read a card your husband gave you when you were dating? This is the reason you saved this stuff, right? Take your pile or box, look at everything—but don't dwell too long—and decide: KEEP IT or TRASH IT. If the KEEP IT pile is huge, it can be subdivided into categories such as: children, husband, high school, college, wedding, trips, or other special events.

Absolute of Organizing: Keep purging simple with Yes and No piles.

Take a closer look. Here's the hard part. You have categorized and purged. If your memorabilia still fills a room...you've got to purge again. Be realistic and ask yourself these questions:
- Have I broken down the items into small enough categories?
- Do I really need to save all of these or can I pick a few representative pieces that are my favorites (such as greeting cards or children's art)?
- Will I ever look at this again?
- Does this item give me a good feeling when I look at it?
- Do I have the room to keep all of this in my house?

DISPLAY YOUR TREASURES

If you've really purged all you can, decide if anything you've discovered today is something you want out on display in your house. Put those items aside. Then decide if you have a place to display them now, or if you need to purchase something like a shelf or frame. When deciding where to display items, group like items together and put up a simple display shelf in the room that makes sense for those items. For example, plates or cups that your children have made or decorated could go in the kitchen.

Absolute of Organizing: Put like things together.

Select the Best Storage Container

Items you don't plan to display will go in a memory box. Think about where you want to keep your memory box and what kind of container you would like. You may already have something appropriate in your home now. If you do not have the right kind of storage, place the items in a regular cardboard box labeled "memories" and put them in a safe place. Now you can go shopping for your own treasure box! This chart offers suggestions on containers that will keep your memories in good shape.

Maintain Your Memory Box

Now that you have a logical place for all your memorabilia, you have to keep up with it. Make sure the containers you have chosen are bigger than what you need right now because you will be adding to them. You can "subtract" from

LOCATION	CONTAINER	FIND IT AT
Bedroom closet	Plastic storage container with a lid	Any home store
Bedroom or family room	Wicker chest	Home décor catalog
	Decorative steamer trunks	Some arts and craft stores
	Wooden hope chest	Furniture store or consignment shop
Basement or attic	Plastic storage container with a lid (be careful of things that will melt in the attic)	Any home store
	Cedar-lined steamer trunk	Any home store

Steamer trunks (right) and stacking storage bins (below) are two options for storing memorabilia.

them each year as well. A great time to go through your memory trunk or box is during a transition time in your life. For my children, I sort their memory boxes at the beginning of every summer. (They are transitioning from one grade to the next.) As for my husband and me, we went through our memory boxes when we moved, when we had a new child, and any time we shifted the function of rooms in our house. You can also go through the box whenever it starts to get over-packed! (I call this the "full barrel" method. You clear it out when it's about to spill over.) Going through it means using the C.P.R. process again. But each time, it's easier and quicker because you have already begun the process of paring down what you want to keep. There are things that mean a lot to you now, but in five years you may wonder, *Why did I ever save this?* Then it's time to throw it out and make room for new memories.

Absolute of Organizing: Subtract before you add.

8. My Collections Are Buried in Boxes

THE PROBLEM

Collections take up a lot of space and collect dust, and they are constantly growing. So how do you organize a collection? You may have a collection and not even realize it. If you buy a refrigerator magnet every time you take a trip, you are a collector. You may think these magnets are practical mementos, and they are, up to a point. But after you have more than ten or so, they are not simply tools, they are a collection.

THE STORY

While working with a client in her kitchen, I discovered a large number of both cookbooks and coffee mugs. She lived alone so I suggested that she keep just a few mugs and only the cookbooks that she regularly used. "Oh no!" she said, "I'm not getting rid of any cookbooks or mugs. I collect them." What I thought was a very practical step became an emotional issue.

People are very passionate about their collections, and as a professional organizer, I have to take that into consideration when coming up with a solution for the clutter.

Practical Collections

I USED TO COLLECT MATCHBOOKS from the restaurants I went to when I traveled. I keep them in my memory box because I don't want to use them and I certainly don't want my kids getting into them. When I decide I no longer want them as a memory, I can put them with my candles and simply put them to good use. They'll go from memorabilia to practical tools.

THE SOLUTION

There are probably as many solutions as there are types of collections. And the solutions for how to keep your collections range from utilitarian to decorative. In order to formulate guidelines for setting up your collections, it will help to answer the following questions for yourself.

What do I collect?

As you sort through your things you may find a collection that you had started a long time ago. Or you may discover you have many similar items and you have become a collector by default. Like the items in your "memory box," it's hard to part with these things and seeing them brings back good memories. If these items are not all together right now, gather them up, box and label until you find a permanent home for them. Whether they are T-shirts, postcards or china figurines, you have to decide what to do with them.

Absolute of Organizing: Keep like things together.

Who do I want to look at this collection?

Think about whether your collection is something your family and friends will enjoy seeing, or if it's something that only you can appreciate.

My matchbook collection helps me remember fun travels I had in my twenties, so I keep it in a private place. If you have something that everyone can enjoy, then it should be on display.

Is my collection practical or ornamental?

The refrigerator magnets and coffee cups are a good example of practical collections. You may want to keep them where you use them—in the kitchen. But if space is an issue, you'll have to keep only a few of these out and store the rest, or perhaps create some kind of display area for them. For example, the coffee cups could be displayed on a simple shelf or in a glass-front cupboard in the kitchen. The magnets could go on their own magnetic board instead of cluttering the front of the refrigerator.

If you need to store a portion of the collection, remember to rotate the items on display to keep the display fresh. Ornamental collections should be out on display. If they are packed away in a box, what's the point of having them?

If you need to store a portion of the collection, remember to rotate the items on display to keep the display fresh.

If it won't be used or displayed, why am I keeping it?

If the answer is that you are saving it to pass down to your children or you'll put it out one day when your children are grown, that's okay. Safely pack it away and label it clearly so it's not forgotten. If your answer is, "I have no idea," then consider selling it or giving it away.

Absolute of Organizing: Keep only what you use.

Where is an appropriate display area?

The answer to this question depends on your home's décor. A seashell collection makes sense in a room that has a nautical flair, or in a bathroom decorated in an ocean or shell theme. Fancy china figurines or plates make sense in a formal dining room or living room. And things like German beer steins would look great displayed behind a bar. Maybe you have a collection that has been packed away for a while because it just doesn't match anything in your home. If you really want to display it, you could consider redecorating a room to match a collection. I had some beautiful Delftware I purchased on a trip to Holland, but I really didn't have a room that matched. When I moved into my new house, I made the living room blue and white and bought an inexpensive white display shelf to hang on the wall. Now the Delftware has a home and I enjoy looking at it every day.

The right case or shelf will help you display your collections.

Take stock, consider future additions. If your collection is finite, then it's a lot easier to pick a place to display it. I'm done collecting matchbooks, so a simple box to fit what I have is fine. If you are still adding to the collection, then you should use a display system that can grow. This is not unlike what you do with your photos. More are coming so you have to plan for them. It may mean purchasing a display shelf that has room left in it, or buying something that you can easily purchase another of as the collection grows.

If you are still adding to the collection, then you should use a display system that can grow.

FIND THE RIGHT DISPLAY CASE, CONTAINER OR SHELVING

Have your collection in front of you in the room where it will be displayed. Now look at the size of it and the colors in it. Whether it's formal or casual, monochromatic or colorful, think about what case or shelving would complement it. I always suggest looking around at what you already own first. If there is nothing that would fit, second-hand shops are a good place to start. Then there's always Internet shopping. If you've got a collection that other people might have too, chances are you'll find some sort of display case online. Simple display shelves that hang on the wall are very popular and can be found in almost any home store. Remember, if you don't like the color of the shelf, you can always paint it!

Custom-made display. If you or someone you know is creative, sketch out what you'd like and see if you can easily make it. My son started to collect mini football helmets a few years ago. Being the way I am, I didn't want them all over his room or crushed in a toy box. So I searched for a display shelf. Finally, I decided to measure their sizes, and figure out how many he would have when his collection was complete. Then my husband put together a simple wooden shelf that I painted and nailed to the wall. Sometimes custom-made is cheaper and easier!

9. The Toys Have Taken Over

THE PROBLEM

If you're a mom, you have children. If you have children, you have toys. And if you come from a large family that gives gifts, you have lots of toys. These toys migrate. They move from basements to family rooms to bedrooms to outside—anywhere your children go.

THE STORY

In our first house, when my husband and I had one child, we had a toy area in the corner of our "breakfast room." Some simple, white, plastic shelving held all of our little girl's toys. Then we had two more children. Once, while we were eating dinner, a basketball went flying across the table. "Maybe we need to rethink the toy area," we both said. So we turned the 8' × 10' (2.4m × 3m) mudroom into the toy room. We decorated it with jungle animals, put up some bigger shelves and added a wooden toy box. It was not large, but it was cute. The older children primarily used it as a place to store their toys. When I was home with the baby, we would lay out a blanket and play on the floor in there. The best feature was a locking door, so when we had company over, we could lock certain toys in and pull out the toys we didn't mind the children using. Now, in our second home, my children have an entire playroom, complete with a sofa, toy bins and a TV. As your family grows, you'll need to adapt your home to your changing needs. You also must be creative with the space and the resources you have.

THE SOLUTION

First, decide where you are going to keep toys in your house. Then decide how you are going to keep them. Finally, develop the habit of doing toy clean-outs at different times of the year. Let's look at each of these three steps and discuss some options in hopes that you will find one that suits your family and your home.

STEP 1—WHERE ARE YOU GOING TO KEEP THE TOYS?

When deciding where to keep the toys, consider the set up of your house and the age of your children, as well as their personalities and play styles. Include your husband and children as you designate your "toy room" or "toy area." If your children are old enough, let them help you arrange and decorate the toy room or area so they feel like they own it. They will be more inclined to help you straighten it up when necessary. It makes them feel "big" and responsible to have their own place. Here are some options to consider when selecting a storage area:

Consider the set up of your house and the age of your children, as well as their personalities and play styles. Include your husband and children as you designate your toy room or area.

Toy room. If you are lucky enough to have a finished basement or an extra room on the main floor of your house, you can designate this as a toy room. It will be the room that your children gravitate to during most of the day. Many mothers say they have a basement that they'd like to use as the toy room, but their children are young and they don't want to be alone there while Mommy is upstairs. In that case I say switch your plan. Maybe the basement can be used as the adults' recreation room or home office and the children can have a room upstairs for play. Also, realize that as they get older, your children may want to be downstairs with the door closed. You can rearrange the rooms at that time. The great thing about having one toy room is that even if it has toys all over the floor, you can write it off as "that's the kids' room" and the rest of your house can still look nice.

Children's bedrooms. If you don't have an extra room to devote to toys and playtime, then you may have to use your children's bedroom as the toy area. In this case you will have to be very conscious of limiting toys and keeping them in proper containers, leaving room for a bed and dresser. Luckily, most children do not have many clothes that need to be hung up so you can devote at least a portion of closet space for toys.

Family room. If the bedrooms are tiny and there are no extra rooms in your house, you may have to use part of your family room to keep toys. This may not be your first preference, but it is a reality for many people. How you arrange the room and what containers you use will be key in keeping this room from looking sloppy or cluttered.

A large closet. You could always use a large closet for storing toys. The children can take out what they want to play with, use it in any room of the house, and when it's time to straighten up, put it back in the closet. Again, with this option the containers you choose and the use of space in the closet will be key to keeping it functional.

Combination of options. If you choose to keep toys in more than one of these areas of your house, I recommend you still use the idea of "keeping like things together" and break down all toys into subcategories. Games could go in the family room, action figures in the bedrooms, stuffed animals in the bedroom and arts and craft supplies in a closet. The last thing you want is to have all types of toys in several rooms of your house. Then it is hard to put things away and keep track of what toys you have.

Absolute of Organizing: Keep like things together.

STEP 2—WHAT WILL YOU USE TO KEEP THE TOYS ORGANIZED?

Once you have designated where you will keep the toys, bring all the toys to that spot. This will help you see how much you need to get rid of to make it all fit. Use the C.P.R. (Category, Purge and Rearrange) process and categorize the toys into smaller groups such as: action figures, stuffed animals, games, puzzles, arts and crafts, kits with small pieces (e.g., building blocks, train sets, etc.) and sports equipment. Once you have categorized, decide what can be purged. Anything that is broken or dangerous should be trashed and anything that your children do not play with anymore can be given away. Now look at what's left and begin to consider what containers you can use to store them. Here are some storage container options to consider:

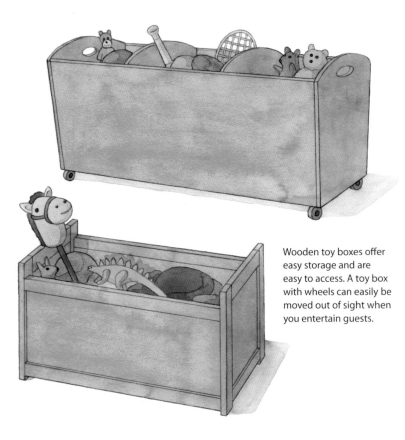

Wooden toy boxes offer easy storage and are easy to access. A toy box with wheels can easily be moved out of sight when you entertain guests.

Wooden toy box. The good old-fashioned toy box is great for big toys that you want out in the open and accessible for the children. They look fine in a bedroom or living room. If you want your living room to have a more sophisticated look when you entertain guests, a toy box on wheels makes it easy to hide the toys in another room for an evening. Be careful not to overfill these, or toys will get broken. These are not great options for little pieces, which tend to fall to the bottom. The benefit—having one box for general toys makes for easy clean-up.

Wooden bookshelf. Bookshelves are great for play sets such as farms or doll houses, which have small pieces inside. They also are great for boxes and puzzles or games, which can be stacked. If your children are climbers, you must make sure these shelves are secured to a wall. The shelves can be used out in the open or tucked into a closet for storage. And if you find one at a second-hand shop, you can always paint it to match your décor.

Toy shelves with plastic bins are great for storing small toys your children frequently play with.

Metal utility shelf. Metal utility shelves are nice and sturdy and usually wider than a typical bookshelf. Use these in a basement or a room that's not a common area in your home because they're not the most attractive storage option. But like the wooden shelves, these can hold play sets, puzzles, games and smaller bins full of toys. Also make sure these are secure for young climbers.

Toy shelf with small plastic bins. Many companies make toy shelves with small, plastic bins that come in pastels or bright primary colors. These shelves are good for small toys that you want your children to access. It is difficult to keep the categories straight, but you can always try to teach your children what toys go in which bins. Labeling the bins with pictures and then words as the children get older is one way to help. Bins are a great option for a toy room or child's bedroom but I wouldn't recommend them for a family room, unless they can be tucked away in a corner.

Large plastic container with lid. When your child has a collection of character or brand-related toys, large containers come in handy. If the containers are clear, children can easily see what's inside. If they're not clear, label the containers with the logo for that toy. You'd be amazed at how early a child can recognize logos for their toys! These bins are typically used for storage and a closet or cabinet is the best place to keep them. But if you must have them out in the open, consider decorating the sides with acrylic paint from an art store.

Large plastic tub. If you have many toys in one specific category such as stuffed animals, an open plastic tub works well. My children always liked cleaning up with tubs because it was like a basketball game. Since tubs are plastic and colorful, I recommend using them in a child's bedroom or out of sight.

Baskets. Like the big open tubs, large baskets can store a lot of one type of toy. However, the baskets are a little more decorative, and they don't look bad in a family room. Small baskets can be used to hold hand-held toys, like the ones found in children's meals at fast-food restaurants. I have a basket in my basement near the back door. When we go for a car ride or to church, I tell the children they can take one or two hand-held toys with them. The toys are usually inexpensive, so if we leave them somewhere it's not a problem. Also, I clean this basket out whenever it gets full. These are the types of toys children rarely miss.

Stuffed animal hammock. These can be found at most toy stores and they are a great option if you want to use the stuffed animals (or any soft toys) as a decoration in a bedroom or toy room.

Clear plastic stackable bins. These bins work well on a shelf or in a closet. They are great for holding smaller toys or arts and craft supplies. If you want the small pieces out of reach for little children, put these bins on top of the shelf or closet so only you can take them down. And if you're catching on to my trend here, I would never leave these out in the open in a family room!

Under-the-bed plastic container. When space is at a premium, you have to use all available options. Under the bed is one of them. Most children use that option anyway, although not in an organized fashion.

There are some nice under-the-bed rolling containers that you can find at home stores or in home improvement catalogs. Limit each under-the-bed box to housing one category of toys and make sure your child knows what is stored in each.

Decorated cookie or popcorn tins. Here's an option for recycling something you may already have—tins. The tins are nice for keeping collections of little pieces together. Make labels for the outside of the tins so your children can identify the toys inside. Depending on how decorative they are, you can keep these out on a shelf or in a closet or cabinet in any room.

Steamer trunk. I love the steamer trunk as a storage option because it can always double as a coffee table. If your children have "dress-up" clothes, this is a great place to store them. However, I have one friend who is a real minimalist and all of her children's toys fit into one steamer trunk. So it could be used in place of a general "toy box." A steamer trunk can be used in any room of the house as long as it doesn't look out of place.

Over-the-door or over-the-closet-bar shoe racks. Shoe racks can be found in home stores or home improvement catalogs. Some toy companies actually make them for dolls or action figures. They are great for special toys that you want to keep nice and don't want thrown into just any container. These racks work well in a child's bedroom or a toy room.

STEP 3—HOW DO I KEEP ALL THESE TOYS STRAIGHT?

In Part I, I wrote about taking a little time each day to get things back to the right place. Involve your children in this process as early as you can. After they're done playing with a group of toys and they're on to the next thing, ask them to help you put the toys back in the right bin. This might be more realistic if your children are small and you are the one supervising their playtime. Once your children are playing independently, you can do a clean-up at the end of the day before bedtime. Ask them to get the toys back to the toy room or toy area. For some that is enough. If you really want to get organized at the end of the day, ask each child to put one type of toy away, so one child would put all the blocks in a bin, another child can put the balls in a tub and another child can help you put away the paper and crayons. Children usually respond better to specific instructions like this rather than a general, "Clean up the toy room!"

Even though you may be cleaning *up* the toys on a regular basis, there comes a time to clean *out* the toys. Here are some options for how and when to make that happen:

Go Through the Toys with Your Children

If you clean out toys with your child, two weeks from now when he or she asks, "Where's my...?" you can say, "Remember, we gave it away to your cousin because you're too big for that now." Or, "Remember it was broken so we threw it out. But now you have a nice, new toy instead."

If the child is involved, I try to make it a simple decision by asking, "Do you play with this anymore?" Then we make a "Yes" and "No" pile. The "Yes" pile goes back in the toy box, on the shelf, etc. Then I deal with the "No" pile on my own. Sometimes I have a specific person I can give a toy to, sometimes there's a charity that I know will take it, and sometimes it's wise to trash it.

Absolute of Organizing: Keep purging simple with "Yes" and "No" piles.

The other good thing about the toy clean out is finding toys you forgot you had. It's like when Woody says in *Toy Story 2*, "Remember to rotate the toys at the bottom of the toy box." For children, it's as good as getting a new toy. If you have more than one child and they each have separate toy areas or toy boxes, I recommend sorting the toys with one child at a time. That way you avoid debates among them over what to keep.

Go Through the Toys Without the Children Around

Most of us will agree that this method is much faster and we'll get rid of a lot more if we just do it ourselves. However, there are often consequences to pay. If you do the clean out and are getting rid of some toys, I would recommend putting them in a holding zone. A "holding zone" can be a black bag or box where you will keep the toys that are going away unbeknownst to the children. You will hold onto them for about two weeks just in case someone is looking for a missing toy. If they absolutely insist on finding that toy, you discretely take it out. Whatever they don't ask for in two weeks should be safe for removal.

MAINTAINING YOUR TOY SYSTEM

If things have gotten out of hand and there are toys all over the house, it's time to "bring it all in." I call this the "Great Toy Clean Out." I bring all toys into one large, open room and begin to categorize, purge and rearrange once again.

When to Maintain

- Before a child's birthday
- Before Christmas/Hanukkah
- Before a change in season like winter or summer—especially for outside toys or toys that may be kept in the garage or shed
- When you are redecorating or rearranging a room with toys in it
- Before a move
- When it all seems out of control!

10. So Many Clothes, but Nothing to Wear!

THE PROBLEM

With clothes there are a variety of problems that might prevent you from keeping them organized. I find most people say space is an issue. Either the closet space is too small, or the dressers are too small. I have even worked with people who have no dressers in their bedroom. Then there's the chore of putting summer and winter clothes away when they are out of season. Add children's clothes into the mix and you've got the problems of random growth spurts, hand-me-downs, and clothes they simply won't wear. And your husband...well, hopefully he's someone who can take care of his own clothes. If not, treat him like one of the children when it comes to organizing solutions.

THE STORY

I recently read a newspaper article about the rising need for junk dealers—the people who come to your house and haul out the big items you want to get rid of but can't throw in the trash. A woman called one company because she literally had clothes piled from floor to ceiling in every room. The only place she had to sit was a portion of her living room sofa! She finally called for help because she

Having Trouble Deciding?

IF YOU FIND YOURSELF NOT ABLE TO PART WITH CERTAIN CLOTHES, think about your goal or motivation for getting organized. Think practically. There are so many charities that take clothing. Why are clothes sitting in your drawers or hanging in your closets if you don't wear them? Ask yourself, "Am I ever going to wear this again?" Honestly answer that question and put it in the right pile.

In giving advice about simplifying your wardrobe, Sarah Ban Breathnach poses this question in her book *Simple Abundance*, "What if everything hanging in your closet were something you loved—something that made you look beautiful or made you feel wonderful when you put it on? Think of how good you would feel every day."

didn't have anywhere to live in her house. I hope that your clothes are not taking over your home, but if they are on their way, let's talk about some solutions.

THE SOLUTION

The best solution to the clothing problem is for you and your husband to set a good example for your children. Start by organizing your own clothes, first.

Organize Mom and Dad's Clothes First

1. Gather all of your clothes on your bed. This includes emptying your dresser and bringing in any plastic bins from the attic. Now you can use the space around your bed for stacking or making piles. Put a clean sheet

on the floor so your clothes won't get lint on them. I suggest you start with folded clothes, then deal with the hanging clothes.

2. Make two piles—"Yes, I Wear It" and "No, I Don't Wear It." Go through every piece of clothing on your bed and make a quick decision.

Absolute of Organizing: Keep purging simple with Yes and No piles.

3. Now go through this process of making Yes and No piles with all of your hanging clothes and with your shoes.

4. Once you have decided what you're not keeping, bag it or box it up and get it out of your bedroom. Put it in a place in your house where you will remember to call to have it picked up, or put it in your car so you will remember to drop it off at a clothing collection center.

5. Now you are left with all the clothes that make you look great and/or feel wonderful! It's time to break down the categories even further. You can make nice folded piles back on your bed. Here are some possible clothing categories:

- T-shirts
- Short-sleeved tops
- Long-sleeved tops
- Shorts
- Skirts
- Blazers
- Suits
- Sweaters
- Exercise wear
- Dress pants
- Blouses
- Pajamas

Absolute of Organizing: Organize from big to small.

6. Take a look at the piles and see if you have way too much of one category. Ask yourself, "Do I really need all these?" If not, purge some more.

7. Decide whether you can keep all of these clothes in your current dresser and/or closet. If not, put the out-of-season clothes in a plastic bin with a lid. Label the bin and find a storage area where it will fit.

8. If you need to update your bedroom with more appropriate clothing storage, see *Options For Storing Clothes* on pages 109.

9. To reward yourself after all this hard work, put on a newly-discovered outfit and go out. Just don't go shopping for clothes!

Organize Your Children's Clothes

1. Start with the oldest child's clothes because they typically don't have any hand-me-downs. Have the child with you to try things on or at least hold them up to see if they still fit.

2. Bring all the clothes into the child's bedroom if you have the clothes stored in other places. Take the clothes and shoes out of the drawers, bins or closets and begin making these piles:

   - *Yes*. The clothes fit, are in good shape and are worn regularly.
   - *Hand-Me-Downs*. These clothes no longer fit, but they are in good condition and will be handed down to a younger sibling or friend of the family.
   - *Donations/Charity*. These clothes can be given away. They must be in fairly good condition and no longer fit your children.
   - *Trash*. These are clothes that are so badly stained or worn that they should not be given to charity.
   - *Memory clothes*. I know this sounds like an odd category for clothes, but I know several mothers who save special clothes or accessories. An example might be a child's Christening dress/outfit or the outfit they came home from the hospital in, or a special bib that was handmade by an aunt. Call these what they are: memorabilia. You want to save them but you're not going to use them again. So package them up nicely and put them with the child's other memorabilia. Just make sure you are not saving too much and try to limit it to really special garments.

3. Put the trash pile in the trash. Bag or box up the hand-me-downs and move them to the other child's room. If they fit now, put them in with

current clothing. If they will fit later, label the box or bin with the size and season of clothes and tuck it in the closet. Next take the donations and move them to your car for delivery later.

4. Take the Yes pile and separate these into smaller piles such as:

- Hanging clothes
- Underwear
- Socks
- Short-sleeved shirts
- Long-sleeved shirts
- Shorts
- Pants
- Pajamas
- Shoes
- Sweat pants
- Sweat shirts
- Sweaters

5. Now look at the dresser and closet and decide if all the clothes will fit. Make a decision about whether you need a larger dresser, or a closet organizing system. Look at the number of shoes and decide where they will be kept as well.

OPTIONS FOR STORING CLOTHES

Dresser. My first option is always a dresser. If you need a new one and have limited funds, second-hand shops are great. You can buy a dresser there and paint it whatever color you want. If you can afford it, buy a good quality dresser that you or your children can use for many years. It's a worthwhile investment.

Basic closet. If you decide to store all the clothes in the closet, first see if you can use what you have, which is typically a hanging bar and a shelf. If you need more hanging space, purchase a double hanging bar, which hangs from the upper bar and increases your hanging capacity by 50 to 100 percent depending on how wide it is. For the children, you could always hang out-of-season clothes up top and current clothing on the bottom bar.

Custom-made closet. There are a number of options for closet organizers. You can purchase anything from a $20 rack system at a home store to custom-made shelving from companies that specialize in closets only. Before you spend too much on a custom closet, remember that children's clothing sizes change quickly, so the configuration should be flexible enough to accommodate larger clothing.

Also, look at what you have to put into the closet first (i.e., the stacks you just made) to determine what you need to store them. If you only need one simple shelf, consider putting it up yourself to save time and money. Don't make the common mistake of letting someone else design the closet while you try to make your clothes fit in.

Shoe Racks. Look at the number of shoes you have and find a floor rack or hanging rack that will work. You can purchase back-of-door hanging racks, wide floor racks, shoe carousels, under-the-bed rolling bins or fabric shoe racks that hang in the closet.

Short shoe racks work well inside a closet.

WHEN TO DO THE CLOTHES CLEAN OUT

Obviously this is a project that does not happen weekly or even monthly. Children don't grow at the same time every year so you need to be flexible. Here are some suggested times of the year to clean out your clothes:

- At the change of a season. Figure out who needs bathing suits, flip-flops and sandals before summer starts. See who needs new school clothes in the fall. And who needs boots, coats or snow pants before the first snowfall.
- Whenever you or your child is consistently having trouble finding something that fits.
- When you or your husband start a new job that requires a wardrobe change.
- When you feel like your drawers or closets are overflowing or so jammed you can't close them.
- When you are moving to a new house.

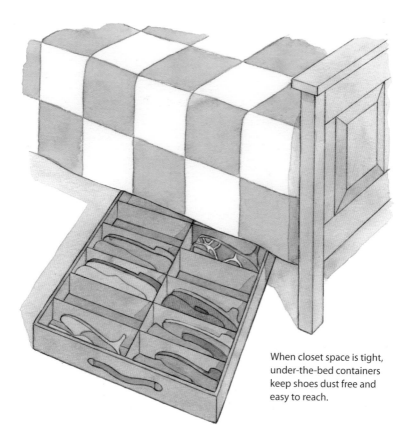

When closet space is tight, under-the-bed containers keep shoes dust free and easy to reach.

11. Where to Put All Those Odds and Ends?

THE PROBLEM

We've talked about all the major categories of things in your house, from clothing to toys to paperwork, but what about those annoying little things that can really clutter a room? Sometimes those odds and ends can accumulate and we just don't know where to put them!

THE STORY

While I was helping a client organize her family room, we needed to vacuum the rug. The vacuum was upstairs in one of the bedrooms. When we finished vacuuming I asked, "Where do you keep this?" Her answer was a blank stare. The vacuum had no home. It just remained in the room where it was last used. We quickly rearranged the family room closet and made a space for the vacuum. The closet was logical because it was a central location in the house.

THE SOLUTION

In order to truly have a "place for everything," you must identify those items in your house that don't have a permanent home. To do this, take a walk through your house and play the game of "one of these things is not like the others." This will help you identify what doesn't really belong, like a sewing needle and thread in the kitchen, or a vacuum in the bedroom, or gifts that need to be wrapped on the office floor. Gather those items together and think about the most logical place to keep them. Here are some examples of mini-categories you might encounter and some options for where to keep them.

Wrapping Paper/ Ribbons

Most moms have wrapping paper and ribbons on hand at all times because you never know when someone will need to go to a birthday party. There are several wrapping paper organizers available ranging from hard plastic stand-up bins to soft vinyl totes. You also could create an organizer for yourself out of a box from a liquor store. These boxes have dividers for bottles that work just as well for large rolls of wrapping paper. You can remove some of the dividers to make space for ribbons, scissors and tape.

Assemble and contain your wrapping materials and find a home for them. Think about where you usually do the wrapping. Is it in the den, your bedroom or in the living room? Find a closet in or near that room that has enough space for the container you choose. Make the decision to keep wrapping paper there and let the whole family know where it belongs.

In order to truly have a "place for everything," you must identify those items in your house that don't have a permanent home.

Extra Gifts

If you have the luxury of a completely empty closet or empty shelf in your home, you can shop in advance for gifts on hand, ready to be wrapped. One of my clients devoted an entire custom closet in her office for just this purpose. Another client used one shelf in her linen closet for extra gifts. With this category, you really need to adapt to your living space. No extra room in the house means no extra presents. However, it is a good idea to look at your monthly calendar and consolidate your gift shopping for the month. If you only have a handful of presents to buy, you could probably find a place to stash them. With little children in the house, it's best to keep these out of sight so curious hands don't open the gift prematurely! Like any of the big categories, have all the gifts in one place so you remember what you have! Decide where this will be: your linen closet, an empty closet, your bedroom closet or in the attic (if it's climate controlled) and don't tell the family! Let this one be your little secret.

Adapt to your living space. No extra room in the house means no extra presents. However, look at your calendar and consolidate your gift shopping for the month!

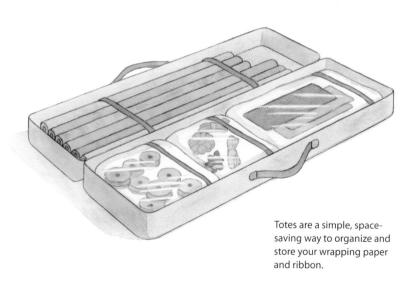

Totes are a simple, space-saving way to organize and store your wrapping paper and ribbon.

Items That Need to Leave the House

This category could include mail, donations, things that are going to a friend, or items you want to return to a store. Store your outgoing items:

1. *In your car.* There's nothing like going right to the finish line. Put the items on your passenger seat so you see them every time you get into the car. Visual reminders are great.

2. *On a table near your door.* Put the items you need to send out in a place you walk by every day. Let them stick out like a sore thumb so you'll return them soon. If you tuck them away, you're more likely to forget about them.

3. *In your bedroom.* Put the items in a place where you will see them every day when you wake up. One of these days you'll remember to write "do returns" in your planner, and then you can have the satisfaction of checking it off your list.

Items That Need to be Fixed

If you leave a broken item exactly where it sits, you might never fix it. You may have a craft table in your home or a work bench in the garage where you do your "fix its." If your fix-it area is crowded, plan some time in your day to do these little projects. You'll be amazed at how quickly some can be done. Include toys and gadgets that need batteries in this area. Keep the supply of batteries close at hand as well as a container for battery recycling. If you don't know where to recycle your batteries, try your township or city's department of public works.

If something needs to be taken out of the house for repair, put it in the "going out" area mentioned previously.

Put together a little box of tools you use most often, such as: masking tape, a hammer, nails, a Phillips head screwdriver, a flat screwdriver, glue, and scissors.

Limit Your Returns

AFTER SEEING MANY CLIENTS OF VARIOUS INCOME LEVELS, I have come to this conclusion: the more you shop, the more you return. I experienced this myself after we moved into our new house. Right after the move, I did a lot of shopping for home items. Before that, I didn't consider myself a big shopper. I mostly bought what I needed and avoided the mall like the plague. The more I picked up, however, the more returns I had. A pile started to grow in my garage, my car and my bedroom. Now that we're settled, the piles have vanished.

So if you are a frequent shopper, you probably have a number of things in your home that need to be returned. Your returns also show you how detailed a shopper you are. If you are returning household things for size, make sure you measure next time. If you return things for color, take a sample of what you are trying to match. If you are returning a lot of clothes, make note of the new size you or your children need. A little planning can save you a lot of time on returns! If you think you may need to take something back, be sure to keep the receipt with it until the decision is made.

Tools You Use All the Time

There are certain tools we moms seem to use all the time. It makes sense to have a small household toolbox easily accessible especially if most of your tools are in the garage, shed or basement. Put together a little box of what you use most often, such as: masking tape, hammer, nails, Phillips head screwdriver, flat screwdriver, glue and scissors. Then find a convenient place for your toolbox; possibilities include a kitchen drawer or closet, the linen closet or a hall table. I use an old lingerie dresser that has several little drawers. It's in the hallway on the second floor and it holds tools, batteries, extension cords and light bulbs.

Cleaning Products

I learned early in motherhood that cleaning products should be kept up high, out of the reach of little children, yet I still go into many homes where cleaning products are kept under the kitchen sink. Even with safety latches, this is dangerous. Save yourself the trouble of installing latches and simply switch your cabinets around. No matter how small your house, there's a high cabinet or shelf where you can keep cleaning products. If you want cleaning supplies in your kitchen, try putting pots and pans or plastic ware under the kitchen sink because these are items that children can play with and then move the cleaners up to high shelves. Another option is in a laundry room or linen closet on a high shelf. Limit the number of cleaners you have so they don't take up as much room. If you want to separate the cleaning products, keep laundry cleaners in the laundry room, household cleaners in a central closet (like the linen closet) and kitchen cleaners in the pantry or a kitchen cabinet.

You can really spruce up a room by simply changing the pictures on the walls and the items on the shelves.

Pictures and Display Items

If you feel as if the pictures or display items in a room are mismatched, take them all down. Now look at what you have and group like things. You might group by color scheme or frame color or theme. My daughter's room became cluttered with all her accumulated knickknacks, so we decided to organize them. We found that she had a lot of blue items and pink items. So we decided to put the blue items on a new, wooden display shelf and the pink items on top of her bureau. Another time she chose to put ocean objects on her display shelf for the summer. The fun thing about knickknacks and display items is that you can change them whenever you want. The items you don't display can be tucked away and brought out at another time. You can organize pictures and display items room by room, or if you want a dramatic change, do your whole house at once. You can really spruce up a room by simply changing the pictures on the walls and the items on the shelves.

Gift Certificates and Gift Cards

One of my pet peeves is people who never use their gift certificates. Why don't they use them? Usually because they can't find the certificate or they don't make a plan to use it. If you think of gift cards as money, put them right in your wallet. When you're at that store and you open your wallet to pay, you'll see the gift card and use it. Or you can keep gift cards and certificates in a special place such as your top desk drawer or your planner as a "to do." Make a note in your monthly list area to go a certain store or make an appointment to use the gift certificate. Keep track of any gift certificates your children receive by keeping the certificates in one location.

Children's Artwork

Here's a category that seems to have a life of its own. Depending on how creative you and your children are, you can accumulate one to five pieces of kiddy art per day for each child. No mother wants to trash her child's creation but then again not many moms have room for all that creativity. The key is balancing sensitivity and realism. You want to treasure your child's creation but you must be realistic about how long to keep each piece. Here are some options:

Display it ...

- On the refrigerator, but limit it to one creation per child. Make it an art gallery that gets updated on a regular basis.
- On a cork board or bulletin board in the play area or a child's bedroom.

- In a plastic box frame if it's a really good drawing or painting.
- On a display shelf if it's a sculpture or chunky piece of art.

Stash it...

- In a desk drawer or in a plastic container under the child's bed if there's no room to display it. When the drawer or container is full, or at the end of the school year, sort through the artwork and decide what to keep and what to trash.
- In a portfolio labeled with the child's name and year.
- In a memory box if it's a piece of art that was done a while ago but is "a keeper."

Trash it...

- Once it has had its time on display.
- If it's a sculpture that has deteriorated or gone bad (like a macaroni necklace).
- If you have multiple versions of the same drawing, painting or art piece.
- After the child has decided he or she no longer likes it or wants it.

Take One Step at a Time

No matter where the paperwork, photos, collections, toys and clothes are in your house, you can begin to shrink the clutter and confusion by tackling one category at a time.

REMEMBER

- Use the C.P.R. method: Categorize, Purge and Rearrange.
- Create a filing system for paperwork you will reference.
- Sort mail and papers every day. Divide it into three categories: TO DO, TO READ and TO FILE. All else is trash.
- Decide how you want to keep your photos and start using that system from this point forward.
- Gather all your memorabilia and find a home for it that allows you to reminisce whenever you want.
- Put your collections on display.
- Decide where toys will be kept in your house and choose storage containers that match your home décor.
- Go through toys and clothes several times a year and weed out what you and your children don't use.
- Once the big categories have a home, find a place to keep the little things that can clutter your house.

Now that your belongings are organized and under control, you can turn your attention to each room of your house. Read on for more ideas on how to create an organized home.

Part III: Organize Your Home

THE COMFORTS OF HOME. A mother's touch is what makes a house a home. I believe part of a mother's job is to organize the home into comfortable, functional rooms. We don't have to do it all by ourselves, but we moms do have to orchestrate and maintain the organization. If you have your time management skills honed, and you have pared down your possessions to what you need, use and love, it's time to tackle the organization of your entire home!

All organizing starts with a decision. To organize the rooms in your house, you have to decide the function of each room first. Once you know the function, you can decide what belongs in or out of that room. Then you can begin to arrange each room to create a functional and relaxing environment for your entire family.

"We shape our dwellings, and afterwards our dwellings shape us."

—**WINSTON CHURCHILL**

12. Where Do I Start?

THE PROBLEM

The whole house is in disarray, and you've made a decision to get organized this year. There are many reasons to organize the entire home: moving into a new house; welcoming a new resident (new baby, aging parents, a homeless sibling); selling your home; or wanting a fresh start from the years of accumulating clutter. Organizing the entire place can be overwhelming. The disorganization took years to accumulate, so how can you turn it around in just a few months?

THE STORY

My family moved about two years ago. We had lived in our previous house for twelve years, so to say I was comfortable and functional where I was living is an understatement. Moving is a time of great change and upheaval that can send even the most organized mom into a tizzy. After two years in our new home, I can see a big difference between our house and the houses of friends who also moved that year. We chose the "room-by-room" approach while others went with the "all-at-once" approach. We like to balance our schedule with house projects and downtime. Some people are always working on their houses, every evening and weekend. Some husbands end up writing checks to contractors while the wife orders the products and services. My husband and I have a "Home Projects Plan" that we often refer to. We look at costs, juggle priorities and schedule the projects before we jump into them.

THE SOLUTION

The first thing you'll need is a plan. If you don't know where to start, go through every room in the house with your spouse (and maybe even the children). Discuss how your family will use each room. In other words, identify the three most important functions of each room. If you add more than three functions, the room may become chaotic and crowded. Some functions are more obvious than others—bedrooms are for sleeping and the kitchen is for eating and cooking. But think about your day-to-day life and be realistic. You might like to watch TV in your bedroom or have the children do homework in the kitchen. These details will affect what is contained in each room and how you will organize it.

As you walk through the house, take notes on what you need to do in each room. Create a "Home Projects Plan" book using a simple notebook. Have a separate page for each room and write down everything you want to change in that room. The plan should include both organizational projects and home improvements. Write it all down, from adding an electrical outlet to buying new window treatments. If you browse catalogs or home improvement magazines, cut out pictures of what you like and put these alongside your "to do" items. This book is a centralized plan of what needs to happen so you can have your dream home.

Where there's a will, there's a way and where there's not, there are excuses.

You may not have any ideas for a certain room right now, other than "clean it out." That's okay. Sometimes when you clear away the clutter, it's easier to envision a room updated and decorated. You may be able to work with what you have in your home and just rearrange. If not, you may need to purchase furniture or hire contractors to really get your home in shape. It all depends on how far you want to take it.

Absolute of Organizing: Start with a good list.

Estimate Your Costs

After you've written down all of your plans, estimate the costs. This may be as easy as pricing something in a catalog. For contracted services like plumbing and electricity, you will want to get at least three quotes. My husband and I tend to go with the middle range of costs unless one of the contractors is significantly better than the others in terms of quality or customer service. Many times you just have to choose whomever you feel more comfortable with. Consider purchasing items yourself such as lighting and plumbing fixtures and then hiring someone to install them. This can often save you money. Once you have all your quotes, you can ballpark the cost of completing each room. It will come in handy when you are prioritizing which room to do first.

Know Your Budget

Budgeting is a step that many couples skip. If you're lucky enough that cost doesn't matter, then you can keep going until your whole house is done. But most families have to work within a budget. You don't want to be in the middle of a big project and suddenly find you are out of money. When we moved into our new house, we knew there were some immediate fixes to be done. We looked at our annual income and expenses and figured out how much we could put aside for home improvements. When the money was gone, we had to stop. We were realistic about how much we could do in that first year.

Another option might be to take out a loan. Whatever your situation, it's important that you and your husband are in agreement with how much money can be spent in getting your home organized and updated. Decide on the total amount you can spend and then prioritize your projects.

Prioritize

The other purpose of the Home Projects Plan is to help you prioritize. There are different ways to prioritize, and no way is right or wrong. Some common ways to choose which room should be first are by using superlatives such as:

- the worst room in the house
- the most used room
- the most visible room
- the easiest room
- the least or most expensive room to do

Much depends on your personality. Doing the worst room first has its benefits because all else will seem easy. Doing the easiest room first might build your confidence to continue on with other projects. Doing the most used or most visible room first may help you feel that you will at least look organized when you have visitors. Whatever your motivation, choose the first room and stick with it until you've done everything you planned and that you can afford. Roughly plan out the order in which you would like your rooms to be finished. Of course this may change along the way, but it's better to have a plan of where you are going than to have no plan at all!

Absolute of Organizing: Finish one thing before you start another.

Scheduling

Keep the House Projects Plan book in a central location where you and your husband can easily access it. As you plan out your week together, you can refer to this book if your schedule allows a home improvement project. Don't leave all the work for the weekend. Sometimes a project may only take two hours and you could get it done together on a weeknight. Or sometimes a big Saturday project may take some prep work that could be done on Thursday or Friday evening. If you are going to paint the living room on Saturday, you could move furniture, bring in the drop clothes, and put up the painter's tape on Friday night after the children are asleep. Then you can jump right into painting Saturday morning.

When scheduling projects, think about what the children will be doing at that time. If one parent can tackle a job, then the other parent can help by taking the children out of the house. If you both want to do a project, take the children to a friend's house or a grandparent's house. If possible, plan projects for a weekday if all your children are in school and your husband can take a day off. Sometimes you have to be creative if you want to get these projects done.

When your children are old enough, you can involve them in the projects. My four-year-old recently picked up a roller and helped me paint an outside wall! Planning ahead and thinking a project through is often half the battle. Including your children in the process is important because you want everyone in the family vested in the outcome. Use incentives when necessary like, "If you all help clean out the garage on Saturday, we can go out for dinner and a movie that night."

How long will this all take?

Now that you have a good idea of what you want to do, how much it will cost and what services it will involve, you can take a look at the big picture. Many people talk about home improvements and say, "Oh, it never ends!" I disagree. It ends when your comprehensive list is finished and your house is as you wanted it. Sure, circumstances will change, and a new project may be born. If you look at each project as finite then there will be a time when you can sit back and say, "We're done."

If the task of organizing your entire home seems overwhelming, count the rooms in your house. If you can organize one room a day, that's how many days it will take to finish the project. An average size house has ten to twelve rooms. At one room a day, you can finish in two weeks. Or, let's say each room will require a week to organize. Then you'll be finished in three months. If your rooms each require a lot of work, let's say one month per room. You still can estimate that in one year you will have your home exactly as you want it. Not bad when you consider how many years it took to get it the way you didn't want it!

13. I Need a Home Office!

THE PROBLEM

You may be thinking you don't need a home office because you don't work from home. Wrong. Papers are coming at you faster than you can read them. Every one of your children has three phone lists for all their activities. You're making doctor's appointments, paying bills and filling out forms on a weekly basis, and your daughter has just asked you to be her Brownie leader! How are you going to keep it all organized? Every mom needs some sort of home office. No matter the size, the home office is where Mom can get it all together.

THE STORY

Several of my clients have the same problem. They have already set up a home office. For some, it's in their basement. Others have a spare bedroom, others just have a desk in a living room. Once that area becomes cluttered and frustrating to work at, they branch out instead of using C.P.R. (Categorize, Purge and Rearrange) to stay organized. Milk crates with files appear in the dining room, and tabletops start to accumulate piles of papers. These moms assume they need a new piece of furniture or a bigger room to hold it all. What they really need to do is get back to basics.

THE SOLUTION

Whether you need to create a home office from scratch or you have an office that is disorganized, you can follow my Room Organizing Worksheet (page 187) to create your own "Mom Command Center." Start by asking yourself these questions and write down the answers:

What is the function of my home office? Is the purpose of your office to pay bills, send letters, keep files, and hold the family computer? Or will you also be running a home business? Will the children be allowed to use your desk and computer? All these questions have to be answered before you can set up your office in the most efficient manner. Make your decision and write down how you are going to use your office. This will help you focus on what you will need in your office.

What do I like about my current home office? Is it convenient because your office is in the main area of the house so you can work when the children are around? Or is it tucked away so it's nice and quiet? Is it light and cheerful? Does it have beautiful furniture in it? Whatever the case, note the positive points of your office so they remain during your reorganization!

Note the positive points of your office so they remain during your reorganization!

What don't I like about my office right now? Maybe it's that you can't see the top of your desk, or that you lose things easily, or that there are piles of paper on the floor. Be honest and identify the problem areas.

What is in my office now? This is really the "Categorize" step of my C.P.R. process. If things in your office are not categorized, you need to physically move them into piles to identify what is there. If they are already in categories, then take a look around and jot down everything you see. Your categories may include: mailing supplies, bills, computer equipment, family paperwork, and photos. When you make a list of categories, it's easy to identify what doesn't belong.

What do I want to keep in the office? Include in this list not only the categories of items but also the furniture or storage containers that are working well for you.

What, if anything, needs to be added? Do I need to hire someone? Sometimes the answers to these questions are obvious. You may need more file cabinets or a better desk chair. But sometimes you won't know what needs to be added until you dig out from all the clutter. It's okay to leave these two answers blank and come back to them. If you need a contractor to make some improvements to your office, make sure you get three estimates for each service required.

Purge. By process of elimination you have determined what does not belong in your office area. Box these items up if necessary and move them out! This is the "Purge" step of C.P.R. Big items can be stored in the garage or basement until you can get rid of them, or you may need to move things to the appropriate room in your house.

Absolute of Organizing: Subtract before you add.

PUTTING IT ALL TOGETHER

Basic Supplies: A typical home office should include a file cabinet, a desk, a phone, a computer and a printer. Some supplies might be: stamps, a phone book, checkbook, envelopes, tape, stapler, scissors and paper. If you will be running your own business from this office, you may also need to bring in your inventory, reference material, forms, catalogs or shipping materials.

Furniture: Many home businesses involve using reference materials like directories, catalogs or other books. If you need those close at hand, make sure you have a wall shelf or a standing bookshelf. Also make sure you have adequate file cabinets and desktop space for what you do at your desk. If you are going to do scrapbooking or crafts in your office, make sure you have a clear tabletop as well as a desk.

Containers: You may need bins for paper or storage bins for things like crafting supplies. If you are using the desk for your In Box, Bills-to-Pay bin and File bin, make sure you have space for all of them. Stand-up bins or wall-mounted bins are a great way to keep these papers visible and orderly without taking up too much desk space.

Work Within Your Budget

IF YOU DON'T HAVE A DESK, there are options at various price levels:

- You can purchase a new one, custom fit to your needs.
- You can find one in a second-hand shop and fix it up to your liking.
- You can make your own desk from a folding table with file cabinets underneath.

I have one friend who was really creative and made a desk from an old, wooden door and two sawhorses!

If your home business involves inventory that you take with you to clients, it makes sense to have the items in containers that travel well, such as a suitcase on wheels or lightweight plastic bins. If you ship items from your home and don't need to carry them out, you can arrange them on a shelf or in a closet with the shipping materials.

Once you've decided what you need for your office, go shopping online or at an office supply store and bring those containers to your office. Once you're sure you have everything, bring it together and assess the situation. Do you need an entire room or will a portion of a larger room suffice?

WHERE WILL THE OFFICE BE?

A typical home has many options for creating a home office area: a spare bedroom, the corner of your family room or living room, or an area in the basement. Even a spare closet can be turned into an office. I've also noticed that many new homes incorporate a desk right into the kitchen counter space. If this is the case in your house, make sure the kitchen desk area is big enough to meet your needs. Maybe it's just big enough to keep your bills, or it's where your child can do his or her homework. Decide on its purpose and make sure it's equipped for its function.

Wherever you decide to put your office, make sure it's in a convenient place where you will use it. Several clients I know have a desk set up in a basement but then tell me they just don't feel like spending time there. An office area that you don't utilize every day is really of no use.

Think about your habits before you decide if you want your office in the main area of your house or in a tucked away spot where you can retreat to do your work.

HOW WILL YOU SET UP YOUR OFFICE?

To arrange or rearrange your office, think in categories. If your office has multiple functions, create zones for each function. If you are using your office area for managing your household files and running a home business, you need to have separate file drawers or file cabinets for each function. You may even want to have two desks, one for personal and one for business.

If you have a computer and several pieces of electronic equipment, make sure you set them up near a grounded outlet and use a surge protector. Also make sure the computer is in a position that will not have glare from the sun if there are windows in your office.

Think about the flow of paper in your office and set the area up in an assembly line fashion. If yours is an office for managing your home, you could set it up like this:

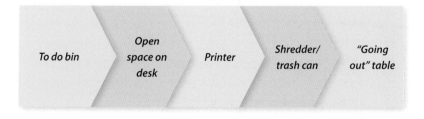

To do bin → Open space on desk → Printer → Shredder/trash can → "Going out" table

If you are also using your office to manage a home-based business, your set up may be more complicated. Many home-based businesses involve taking orders, collecting money, and filling and shipping orders. You can set up stations for each step in the process. Have order forms by the phone or computer, wherever they come in. Then spread them out on a table for filling orders. Keep a record of who has paid and who has not. You could use a letter holder on the table or two bins accurately marked. Have your packaging materials either under the table or in a closet in your office. Once the packages are ready to deliver or mail, have a "Going Out" bin by the door of the office. Your straight-line process might look like this:

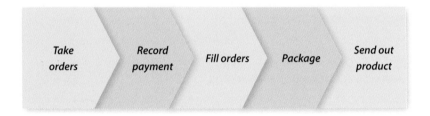

Take orders → Record payment → Fill orders → Package → Send out product

Having your business set up in this way will avoid confusion about where a certain order is, and who has paid. It also helps you see exactly what part of the process you need to focus on at any given time.

Put on the Finishing Touches

Once your office is set up functionally, make sure it also is aesthetically pleasing. When you feel at ease and have a clear space to work, you will have a clear and focused mind to do your work.

- If you like visual reminders and motivators, put up a bulletin board. Post pictures of loved ones, pictures of prizes you are working towards, or simple notes. Bulletin boards do have potential for clutter so make sure you keep them current. Don't cover old notes with new ones.
- If your office is in a corner of a larger room in your house, make sure it blends. You wouldn't want a metal desk in a French Country living room. Try to match the wood tones of the furniture.

- If your file cabinets are visible in your office, also make sure they are wood. Metal or plastic bins should be tucked away in a closet and not out in the open.
- If you have clients come to your office, make sure you have a comfortable place for them to sit, and a clear table for them to use.
- Add something pretty like a vase of flowers, a beautiful picture, or a great smelling candle.

USING AND MAINTAINING YOUR OFFICE

Don't let the children touch. If your home office is going to be used by your children because there is only one computer in the house, make sure your work and important papers are filed away or even locked up when you are finished working. This is a great motivator for keeping your desktop clear! When the children use the computer or materials there, make sure they only have access to what they are allowed to use.

Set a schedule for working your home-based business. If you're lucky enough to have your own office with a door, it's easier to be disciplined about your starting and ending time. When you finish for the day, place everything you need to do tomorrow in your TO DO file and write it in your daily planner, then close the door. If you don't set up boundaries and routines when working at home, it is easy to let your work time spill into family time. If you work while the children are home, communicate with them that you are working and what's expected of them. You may want them to play by themselves or watch a movie, or you may have a baby-sitter there to attend to their needs.

Set time in your schedule to manage the family. For the day-to-day management of a family, it's best to do it every day so it doesn't pile up on you.

- Paying bills is a top priority so it's worth the effort to schedule the time and write it in your planner. You can write it down as soon as you receive a bill, such as "send Visa bill" on the 10th if it's due on the 17th. If you handle all the household bills, set a specific day of the week when you pay them.

You can do this weekly, bi-monthly or monthly if you coordinate the due dates with your utilities and credit cards.

- Phone calls can take up a lot of a mother's time in any given week. Instead of just calling someone when you think of it, make a list on a daily or weekly basis of whom you need to call. Then you can be efficient about your time and call when the house is quiet, perhaps after the children go to school or when the baby is taking a nap. You'd be amazed how many calls you can make in a half hour when you have focused time. Even if you're just leaving messages, you can get your calls out there. If you're in the middle of doing something else, use caller ID or the answering machine to screen your incoming calls. Only answer if you have the time to talk.

> *The secret to maintaining an organized office is to keep all your office materials IN while keeping toys, food, and extraneous stuff OUT!*

- Filing is something you can do in about five minutes per day. If you don't receive a lot of papers to file you may be able to do it once a week. The other method to use is the "full barrel" method, which means when your "To File" bin is full, it's time to file.

- Reading may be another function that can take place in your office area. You can read periodicals for your business or information from school or children's activities. Again, make room in your schedule to read your incoming papers every day and it will only take five to ten minutes. If you let it pile up, not only does it take longer, you'll also be less likely to want to tackle the pile.

- Use your daily planner to keep track of special projects. Try to work on one project per day if possible. You may be shopping for new car insurance, planning a birthday party or decorating a bedroom. Create an action file for each project and pull that file out when you're working on it, then put it away when you're finished for the day.

End of the year clean out. Clearing out your office from year to year keeps it under control. Here are some suggestions for items to clear out:

- Pull out your tax-related information. Total up expenses and income for both personal and business tax forms.
- Review your "Charitable Contributions" folder and total up all those receipts.
- If you're someone who likes to have an idea of where the money went this year, take credit card statements and your checkbook log and categorize your expenses in a simple spreadsheet.
- If you use Quicken or similar software for your banking, create an end-of-the-year report for your budget totals.
- For all reference files, take a look through each one and toss what is outdated or unnecessary.
- Clear out your children's school files at the end of the school year.
- If you have a business that requires you to keep inventory, tally up the cost of that inventory for your taxes. In some cases you may want to have an end-of-the-year sale to clear the shelf.

The secret to maintaining an organized office is to keep all your office materials *in* while keeping toys, food, and extraneous stuff *out*! Do this on a daily or weekly basis so it doesn't pile up, and you will have a functional home business—even if that business is simply managing your home and family.

14. Never Enough Closets or Storage

THE PROBLEM

So many moms tell me they don't have enough closet or storage space. If you have an old home, your closets are probably small and few. You know why? Because they had less stuff in the old days! If you have a newly built home, you may have larger closets and more of them to work with. There are pros and cons to closets in each type of house. While the old houses may have sturdy wooden shelves, closets in the new homes usually have wire racks. Some people have so many closets they can't decide what to put in them and each closet becomes a catchall.

THE STORY

One of my clients has a small house where she and her husband raised six children. Family gatherings were pretty tight at their house after their children were married and had their own children. They built an additional family room with an average-sized closet in it. The original idea for the closet was to hold the coats for guests because the front hall closet was packed. But the new closet actually became a place to put odds and ends that didn't have an obvious place in the house. So after a few years, the closet contained shopping bags, the vacu-

The first step in organizing a room is organizing its closet.

um, games, extra blankets, children's chairs, and small appliances that were only used a few times a year. There also were bags of miscellaneous papers that had been cleared off the dining room table when company came. One of their daughters bought them a closet organizer to help them out. A year later, it was still in the box, buried under the stuff in their closet. Their son opened the door one day and jokingly said, "See, we put the closet organizer in there but it doesn't work."

THE SOLUTION

To truly organize your closets and storage, you've got to determine what storage you have, the functions of each closet or area, what needs to be stored, and what if any additional storage options you need. Use your Home Projects Plan book to help tackle this problem.

To assess your storage areas, take a walk through your house. Is there a usable attic, basement, or crawl space? How about a shed or garage? What about shelves or built-in cabinets in your home? Maybe you have an armoire, an old trunk or tall bookcase that you aren't using. All of these things are potential storage.

Functions of Closets

After you have cleared out the clutter in your house and decided on the function of each room, it should be easy to decide the function of the closets. The first step in organizing a room is organizing its closet. An organized closet allows you to maximize what you store so you can better arrange what is left out displayed. Remember to keep like things together and limit the function of the closet to two or three categories. For instance, a bedroom closet may hold clothes, shoes, and extra linens. A family room closet may hold games, throw blankets, and candles. A closet in the front entrance may hold outerwear, umbrellas, and backpacks for school. This helps prevent the overloaded and overstuffed closet where everything is shoved in and piled high. Even if your closet is bigger than you need, limit the use of it. There's nothing wrong with having space to spare!

Absolute of Organizing: Keep like things together.

What Needs to be Stored?

When we talk about storage, we typically use it for items that we don't need every day, or large items that can't be kept in an average room in the house, such as golf clubs, large "outside" toys, gardening tools, the vacuum, holiday decorations, out-of-season clothes, memory boxes, and camping gear. You may also have unique things to store like inventory for your business, a collection that you haven't decided what to do with, or items that you sell online. Write these items down on your list and then treat it like a matching test, drawing lines from the "What needs to be stored" column to the "Storage Area" column. This chart should address the big categories of things you have as well as those odds and ends that don't seem to fit into any category.

SAMPLE STORAGE CHART:

STORAGE AREA	CONTENTS
Attic	• Holiday decorations • Mom's and Dad's memory boxes • Camping equipment
Cedar closet	• Mom's and Dad's out-of-season clothes • Formal dresses • Wrapping paper and supplies • Sewing fabric
continued on next page	

STORAGE AREA	CONTENTS
Basement	• Tool bench • Painting supplies • Large toys • Arts and craft supplies • Laundry detergents • Dry food and bulk items
Front hall closet	• Hats, gloves, coats • Umbrellas, boots • Video camera • Portable TV for car
Linen closet	• Blankets and sheets • Cleaning supplies • Vacuum • Extra sundries and refills
Garage	• Bikes • Sports equipment • Decorative flags • Pool supplies • Folding chairs • Outside toys • Stroller • Ladders

continued on next page

STORAGE AREA	CONTENTS
Kitchen closet	• Kitchen cleaning supplies • Broom, dry mop • Plastic wrap, foil, sandwich bags • Cookbooks • Lunch boxes and water bottles
Shed	• Lawn mower • Gardening supplies • Wading pool • Wagon • Extra lumber

PUTTING IT ALL TOGETHER

When you start reorganizing a closet, you've got to take everything out. Use the C.P.R. (Categorize, Purge and Rearrange) process and remember that in this case "purging" may just mean moving something to a different closet. Before you rearrange, take a good look at the space you have. Be sure to use it efficiently before placing any items inside. In some cases you may need to temporarily put a category in a cardboard box or bag until you purchase the container or shelf that you want for your closet.

Additional Storage Options

Now that you've decided what's going into a closet or storage area, consider how to fit it all in so that it's accessible. There's always the option of hiring a closet organizer company to come in and custom build shelves and racks. But sometimes it's just as easy (and less expensive) to work with the shelving you have and make minor changes. Here are some quick tips for efficiently using the space in your closets:

Example Layout of a Child's Closet

Memory Box

Sheets and blankets

Clothes to grow into

Shoe organizer

Laundry basket

Toys

Art portfolio

- Put in a second hanging bar that hangs below the one you have for more hanger space.
- Use hanger holders that can fit four or five pairs of pants or shirts, if your horizontal space is tight.
- Use a shelf topper on the top of your closet if you've got extra "head room."
- Use a vacuum-sealed storage bag for bulky items such as comforters and sweaters.
- Modify the wooden shelves you have in a closet to suit your needs. Make a shelf taller or longer by relocating shelves or adding them. You can do this with plywood and a 2' × 4' (61cm × 122m) board or the brace.

If you simply don't have enough closets, then consider furniture that has built in storage. Many companies make pieces of furniture that offer additional storage. If you don't have a front hall closet, you could use a coat rack or a storage bench. If you don't have a garage, then you can use a shed or basement for storing outdoor equipment.

15. The Kitchen Is the Family's Hub

THE PROBLEM

Kitchens come in all shapes and sizes, but their function is basically the same. This is where you cook and eat and entertain guests. And more often than not, this is where you talk on the phone, take messages, help your children with art projects and homework and play scheduling secretary for the family. Given all those functions, there is a lot of "stuff" that can end up in the kitchen by the end of the day.

THE STORY

One of my first clients hired me to organize her kitchen. Like many of the older homes in my neighborhood, hers was not an "eat-in" kitchen but instead had an area for cooking and a separate dining room where the family ate. She told me that the dining room table was usually filled with children's toys and art projects by the end of the day and in order to eat, they moved the clutter onto the floor or pushed it to the center of the table. Her story is not uncommon, especially among stay-at-home moms with pre-schoolers. I wanted to help her create a more serene table for the family meals without cramping her family's easy-going style. The dining room was fairly large so we were able to create zones for the room's many functions. We added a nice activity table for her children to use. We also used shelves in a corner to store the toys. With the dining room table cleared of debris, we dressed it up with a nice tablecloth and vase of flowers. When we finished, the room finally looked more like a grown-up dining room than a playroom.

THE SOLUTION

Determine all the functions your kitchen serves by using my Room Organizing Worksheet (see page 187) to answer these questions:

What do I like about my kitchen? It might be that you like the cabinets or the set up or the size of your kitchen. If so, these are things that you won't have to worry about changing. I believe it helps to focus on the positive so you know it's not a lost cause!

What don't I like about my kitchen? A common concern I hear from my clients is that the counter space is cluttered or the cabinets are so full, things fall out every time they're opened. Or they say there simply isn't enough space in their kitchen. Sometimes that changes just by paring down to what they need, use and love in their kitchen. Decide what it is that you don't like and let that be the focus of your reorganizing efforts.

What is in my kitchen now? You can jot down the categories of stuff in your kitchen just by opening the cabinets. And sometimes one category is the biggest problem and it doesn't even belong in the kitchen! I had one client whose kitchen table was filled with paperwork for a class she was taking. When I asked her where it belonged, she said, "In the office." So we boxed it up and moved it to the office. Kitchen problem solved. Now it was an office issue. It's okay to push these off because when you finish organizing the kitchen, you can handle the office.

Absolute of Organizing: Finish one thing before you start another.

What do I want to keep in the kitchen? Make sure your answer to this question agrees with the functions you've established. And consider this: Even if you use the kitchen table for projects because it's the biggest table in the house, you don't have to store all those materials in the kitchen. Your children can still do their homework at the kitchen table, but keep their pencils, scissors, and glue in a desk somewhere else. When the schoolwork is done, have them put it back where it belongs. Even if you like to sit at the kitchen table to do bills and read the paper, you don't have to keep them there. Clear it off when you're finished so the kitchen can go back to its original purpose: a place to cook and eat.

What, if anything needs to be added to the kitchen? And do I need to hire someone? If there are any obvious changes like a new floor or counter, jot those down now. You can come back to this question on the worksheet once you have categorized and purged. Perhaps you don't have enough room for all your necessities and a new closet or cabinets are needed.

Categorize

Begin this step by pulling everything out of the cabinets so you can see how much of each category you have. This also allows you to take a new look at the empty space in your cabinets; clean them out and start fresh with a new system.

Purge

There may be items that have been buried for years that you didn't even realize you had. You may find broken items. Or you may realize that your Crockpot has been used only as a place to dump odds and ends! If you have three sets of dishes and two are from the 1960s, maybe it's time to part with them. Find yourself a complete set of matching dishes for everyday. Decide how many are reasonable for your family. If you've still got sippy cups and your youngest is in high school, there's another item you can purge. Create a box for trash and one for donations, and then move these boxes out of the kitchen and dispose of them once the kitchen is organized.

Find Convenient Locations

Now that you have what you want to keep in your kitchen and it's categorized, think about how to rearrange these items back into your cabinets and drawers. Start with the items that you use every day. Other items like serving dishes, appliances that are rarely used, and entertaining items like a punch bowl may need to be kept in storage if your kitchen is too small. Leave that decision until the end. If you buy food or paper products in bulk, you will probably need a storage shelf somewhere else in the house to keep those items. Below is a list with suggested locations for the various categories:

- *Everyday dishes*: Place above dishwasher for easy unloading.
- *Glasses*: Keep near the fridge since that's where you use them.
- *Serving dishes*: Keep up high in cabinets as they're not used every day.
- *Bakeware*: Keep where used—near oven or in drawer underneath oven.
- *Pots and pans*: Keep in low cupboards for easy access. These are okay for kids to play with.
- *Kids' plastic dishes and cups*: Keep in low cabinet or drawer so kids can reach them.
- *Baby bottles and baby food*: Keep in high cabinets near stove so kids can't get into them.
- *Dry food and canned goods*: Keep like things together in the pantry or on a lazy Susan. It will be easier to find what you need.
- *Plastic containers*: Keep them where you use them—in a drawer or cabinet near the fridge or under the sink. Take off the lids so you can stack them or buy collapsible ones.
- *Cookbooks*: If used often and in good condition, keep them out in view. If not keep them on a shelf in the pantry or cabinet.
- *Paper products/foil/wraps:* Keep up high in pantry or cabinet to keep the kids out.
- *Lunch boxes/water bottles*: Keep in the pantry or a low drawer or cabinet so the kids can reach them easily.
- *Small appliances*: Keep in low cabinets or pull out drawers for easy access.
- *Entertaining pieces*: Keep in out-of-reach cabinet or in storage since these are only used a few times each year.

Of course you have to consider the age of your children and your family habits when determining what's right for you.

- As your children get older you may want them to be able to get their own snacks and drinks, but when they are young you might want to keep those items out of reach.
- When determining a low or high shelf, think about the weight of objects and what's most comfortable for you to reach.
- If you have a child with food allergies, it's a good idea to put the "bad" foods up high and create a drawer or shelf for his or her special food. This makes it easier for baby-sitters and other family members to know what your child can eat.

MAXIMIZE YOUR SPACE

If cabinet space is a problem, make sure you are making the most of yours. There are several products on the market that can help maximize the space you have. Collapsible or stackable plastic storage containers are a great idea. If you have a lot of "head" room in one cabinet you may want to add an under-the-shelf basket to double up the space.

If you can't reach your mugs, you can install a pull-out mug rack with hooks. A simple wire rack can help you store small plates on top of larger ones in your cabinet. Before you purchase these items, make sure you know which cabinets they are going into and make a list that includes the measurements of the cabinets so you're sure they will fit.

Counter Tops: The golden rule about counter tops is to only have out what you use every day. There's no sense in having a coffee maker on the counter if you don't make coffee every day.

If you're not a cook, then the cooking utensils can go away in a drawer instead of in a crock on the counter. Also, if you've got the space to stash it, then do so. Tuck that dish rack under the sink and put away the toaster oven if you really need the counter space.

Absolute of Organizing: Finish one thing before you start another.

An Organized Fridge Is a Healthy Fridge

This may sound crazy but I even categorize the food in my refrigerator. If you think about it, that's how refrigerators are designed. There's a shelf for drinks, a bin for fruit, a bin for vegetables, a drawer for meats, a shelf for leftovers, a shelf for dairy items and door shelves for condiments. Separating the food this way serves two purposes:

1. You see what you have and therefore what you need.
2. It's easier for you and your children to pull foods from the various food groups when preparing a meal.

If the food is all over the place, items will get buried in the back. Before you know it, you're buying something unnecessarily or opening a new jar of something that's already in the refrigerator. I once cleaned out a refrigerator that had ten half-eaten loaves of bread, five jars of pickles and seven half-gallons of ice cream. In that household, new foods were opened before the old ones were finished. The refrigerator was packed and it was hard to see what was in there. If your refrigerator is so packed you can't fit anything new in, don't go food shopping until you can see some space.

MEAL PLANNING

One way to avoid the over-stuffed, unorganized refrigerator is to look at your left-overs when planning a meal. That's not to say that every night is a "leftover" night (children hate that word). Think of it as a "leftover make over." Look at the pasta, rice or vegetables you have and think about a new sauce to put over them or how you can toss them into a casserole or soup. It's a chance to be creative with your cooking. Once you've chosen your make over item, also make something new to round out the meal. This will keep the meal fresh. Avoid the habit of making a new full meal every night and then having a refrigerator full of leftovers by the end of the week. If you find you have many leftovers no one eats, you may need to make smaller portions for the next meal.

Another way to handle leftovers is to have a "whatever you want" dinner. Pull out what's in the refrigerator and place it on the counter in categories. Then let everyone choose one meat or protein, one starch and one fruit or vegetable.

Snacks: Many nutritionists recommend having healthy "ready snacks" like yogurt, carrots, celery sticks or apple slices placed at the children's level so they can grab them on their own. If you let them know what shelf is theirs, they can decide what food to eat. It only takes a little planning ahead and some categorizing to really have a healthy refrigerator.

Snacks for guests: I have to admit, one of the reasons I like keeping my house organized is that it's never a problem to have visitors. I love the challenge of finding a snack I can whip up from the food on hand. And if I find I don't have a lot of one snack, I use a three-tiered dessert stand or a divided serving tray and just put out a little of each snack. You could use three different types of cookies, chips, crackers, fruit, nuts or candy. If you have half a tray of brownies left from the other day, cut them, arrange them on a plate and sprinkle with confectioner's sugar to make them look just-baked. There's no need to run to the store every time someone comes over to visit. Think about what snacks you like to make and always have those ingredients on-hand.

MAINTAINING YOUR KITCHEN

Once you have set up your kitchen efficiently, you'll need to maintain the organization.

Daily Clean-up Routine

It's easy to spend a lot of time in your kitchen, especially if you have three meals a day at home with the children. To cut back on this time, I have a clean-up routine after each meal. I only hand-wash dishes and sweep the floor after dinner, unless

Stay Organized During a Renovation

RENOVATING YOUR KITCHEN CAN BE VERY DISRUPTIVE to daily living. I recommend that before the contractors come in, you organize what's in your kitchen as mentioned in this chapter. Then you will have a clear picture of what additional storage or counter space you need before you redesign it. Once the contractors are scheduled, take out things that you use every day like utensils, a few plates, mugs and glasses, coffee maker, etc. Place these items in a box or two and mark them "Everyday items." Likewise, take out everything else in your cabinets and put them into labeled boxes. This should be easy to do once your kitchen is organized into categories. After your kitchen is renovated, you can easily take one category at a time and put it back into the correct drawer or cabinet.

there is an exceptional amount of dirt on the floor or dishes in the sink before then. Here's my clean-up routine:

- Have the kids clear their own plates
- Rinse dishes and load the dishwasher
- Put all the food away
- Wipe the table and counter tops
- Run the dishwasher after dinner
- Put clean dishes away in the morning

Once a week, I wipe down the counters and appliances with a disinfectant. During my weekly house cleaning I mop the kitchen floor.

Papers

When it comes to the kitchen, just say no to papers. The only papers you should have in the kitchen are:

- Take-out menus
- Coupons (in a coupon caddy)
- Recipes (in a recipe file)
- A family calendar
- A note pad by the phone
- A perpetual food list on the refrigerator

All other papers should be kept in your home office area.

Refrigerator Art

Keep refrigerator art to a minimum. If you must have photos on the fridge, use a magnetic plastic frame to keep the grease and grime off them. If you hang children's art, use a clip to keep it from flying off with every slam of the door. I also recommend displaying one piece or art per child and rotating it from time to time. If your refrigerator looks like a scrapbook , it's time to start a scrapbook!

16. I Can't Even Walk in the Kids' Rooms

THE PROBLEM

Your child's bedroom was in perfect order when he or she was a baby. You neatly put away his or her clothes every night and picked up any toys and books and placed them on the correct shelf. Before the child arrived you had carefully decorated the nursery to your liking. The curtains, bedding and pictures all matched and it was a peaceful, beautiful room. Then your child grew up. Toys and knickknacks accumulated, posters and unrecognizable artwork appeared on the walls, shoes and socks are forever strewn, and you can't see the rug through all the toys that lie there. Now you just want to close the door and forget about that room!

THE STORY

When I think of really difficult children's rooms, there are a few that come to mind. I hate to say it, but it's the smart, creative children who are the hardest to organize. So take heart: If your child's room is a mess, chalk it up to creativity and intelligence! One room I can think of belongs to a boy whose parents did not own a TV. In his spare time, this child made art projects, read books, did puzzles and played games. (All the wonderful, mind-stimulating stuff our children

> *Your child's bedroom is a place for him or her to sleep, but it may also be the playroom, the art room and the reading room.*

should be doing!) To make matters worse, their house did not have a playroom, so any organizing solutions had to be implemented in his small bedroom.

THE SOLUTION

Think about what activities take place in your child's bedroom. It's a place for him or her to sleep, but it may be more. Like the child in my story, it may also be the playroom, the art room and the reading room. As your child grows older it is a place where he or she can display his or her personality. Once you have the functions, use my Room Organizing Worksheet (page 187) to answer the following questions.

What do you like about the room currently? You may like the furniture and décor in the room but you just can't appreciate it through all the mess. Perhaps you like the size of the room or closet, or maybe there's a particular feature of the room that you like, for instance a window seat. Make sure you keep or enhance the positive aspects of this room as you organize.

What don't you like about the room currently? Most clients I have worked with point to the amount of stuff that fills their child's room, or to the fact that everything is out and nothing gets put away. Whatever it is that you don't like about this bedroom, make it the focus of your reorganization efforts.

What's in the room now? Here's where we get into categories again. If everything is everywhere, begin to make piles on the floor or bed so you can assess what's in this room. Take heart, it will all get put away as part of your organizing project! Some typical categories are:

- Toys
- Puzzles
- Dress clothes
- Art supplies
- Games
- Stuffed animals
- Finished artwork
- Books

- Knickknacks
- Clothes
- Trophies and medals
- Collections
- Finished schoolwork
- Memorabilia

Purge: Look at the categories and pull out anything your child doesn't use or wear anymore. These items can be donated to a charity or handed down to another child. Also get rid of anything that is broken and clothes that are not wearable. Box up these "purged" items and move them out of the room. Then look at your remaining piles. Is there too much of one category? Reason with the child to let go of some things, or decide what the child won't miss and purge it. Refer back to the chapters in Part II for more details regarding clothes, toys, paperwork, memorabilia and collections.

Absolute of Organizing: Keep purging simple with "Yes" and "No" piles.

Rearrange: I recommend organizing from big to small. Now that you have categorized and purged, take a step back and look at the big picture of your child's room. You may even want to use boxes to remove everything to see the whole room without the clutter. Now you can assess your furniture situation.

What, if anything, needs to be added to the room? Do you need to hire someone?

- Does the child have a good-sized dresser for all of his or her clothes?
- Is the closet set up for what it needs to contain?
- Is there a desk in the room so he or she can make art projects, store art supplies and do homework?
- Is the bed the right size for the child? Are there storage possibilities under or around the bed?
- Are there any shelves on the walls for display items (like knick-knacks, collections or trophies)?
- Is there a bulletin board, magnetic strip or plastic frames for displaying artwork?
- Is there a toy box, shelf or bins for all the toys in the room?

Now comes the fun part—you get to go shopping! There are so many options with the Internet, catalogs, second-hand shops and home stores that it doesn't have to be an expensive trip. I believe it's best to know exactly what you're looking for before you go shopping. If your child's room has white furniture and you need to add a desk with some drawers, shop for a white desk with drawers. It's also good to think long-term. If you invest in a full-sized dresser now instead of a tiny baby dresser, you won't have to buy new furniture in five years. And if you purchase a big bookcase now, you can use it for books and stuffed animals. As the child grows he or she can add more books and perhaps keep trophies on top.

The fact is, your child is going to grow and change but the room will stay the same size. Maximize the storage possibilities now so you will have room for the big items later.

Your child is going to grow and change but the room will stay the same size. Maximize the storage possibilities now so you will have room for the big items later.

PUTTING IT ALL TOGETHER

Now that you have identified the categories of what stays in the room, and you have the furniture and containers that are necessary, it's time to put the pieces of the puzzle together. Take the most important categories—the things your child uses every day—and find a convenient home for them. Things that are not used every day can go on higher shelves in the closet or tucked away in bins with lids. Display items that should be seen and not played with can be placed on a wall shelf.

As you arrange the furniture and containers in the room, remember to keep some open space so the child can stretch out on the floor to read or play. A little open space is good for the mind. If he can't move freely in his bedroom, the child

Children's Bedroom

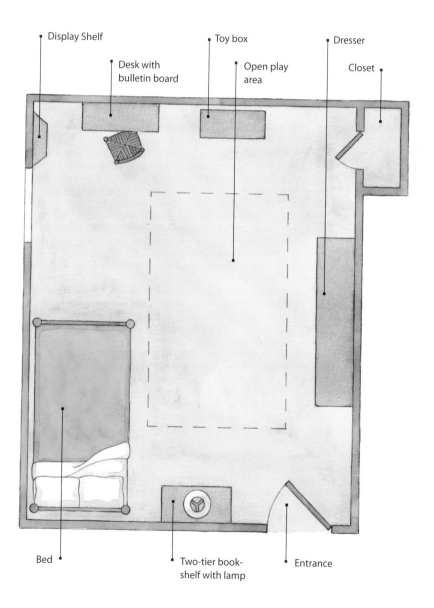

Display Shelf

Desk with
bulletin board

Toy box

Open play
area

Dresser

Closet

Bed

Two-tier book-
shelf with lamp

Entrance

Even little children can have a hand in keeping their rooms straight. The children can pick up their clothes and make their beds in the morning, and then put their toys away in the evening.

may feel frustrated or stifled. If it's a room that is that full of stuff, you really need to think about what you can move out. You may even consider renovations to create more space.

Put Limits on What They Keep

By purchasing containers you are limiting how much stuff your child keeps. If you give him or her a shelf for display items, then once that shelf is full, that's it! Don't fall into the habit of simply buying new display shelves whenever the old ones are full. Instead use the "full-barrel" method—once it's full, clean it off. If your child accumulates little figurines or pieces of nature frequently, you may want to help him or her change the display shelf on a seasonal basis. Just like changing the artwork on your refrigerator door, you have to keep it fresh so it doesn't get cluttered.

Absolute of Organizing: Subtract before you add.

Keep Clean-up Simple

Once your child's room is organized, someone will have to keep up with it. Hopefully that someone is not always you, Mom. Even little children can have a hand in keeping their rooms straight. Remember the daily routines we established in the time management section of this book? The children can pick up their clothes and make their beds in the morning, and then put their toys away in the evening before bed. The simpler the clean-up instructions, the better they are. Every morning, I can be heard saying, "Clean clothes in the drawers, dirty clothes in the hamper." Likewise I say every evening, "Put your books on the book shelf and toys in the toy box." Now doesn't that sound simple? Even a three-year-old can follow simple instructions. Avoid saying things like, "Clean up this room," especially to young children. It's overwhelming to them and they might just fight back or think, "I can't do that." Giving specific instructions that sound easy to do will help them say, "I can do that!"

17. Our Main Bathroom Is Embarrassing

THE PROBLEM

If you have one main bathroom that is used by both your children and anyone who comes to your house, you probably struggle on a daily basis to keep it presentable.

Children leave toys around the tub, gobs of toothpaste on the counter, dirty towels anywhere but on the towel rack, and little boys often "miss" the toilet. (If you know what I mean!)

THE STORY

One of my clients had only one full bathroom in her house. It was used by her daughter as a place to play, which is fine, but I thought about how a visitor would feel taking a shower in a tub filled with toys. I've been in that situation, and before you step foot in the shower, you have to clean up other children's toys. Not something you want to do while visiting another person's home. When I looked at this client's linen closet, which was right outside the bathroom door, there was plenty of room to store the bath toys. We just had to start by cleaning out the linen closet.

Store every bath item you can in your linen closet and only keep the bare essentials in the bathroom.

THE SOLUTION

When considering how to organize your bathroom, you have to take into account what type of linen closet space you have. I suggest you store every bath item you can in your linen closet and only keep the bare essentials in the bathroom.

Take a look at some simple solutions to common bathroom problems by using my Room Organizing Worksheet (page 187).

How do you use your bathroom? While it may seem obvious, the function of your bathroom depends on the number of bathrooms in your house, the size of the bathroom, its location and its storage capabilities. Think about who uses this bathroom and what they use it for. If there is too much going on in your bathroom, maybe some functions like doing hair and makeup can be moved to the bedrooms.

What do you like and don't like about your bathroom? If you have no closet in the bathroom, then you may want to add storage cabinets under the sink. If your medicine cabinet is too small, then consider purchasing a bigger one from a home store. If your bathroom looks too juvenile and you want to redecorate, think about a design that the whole family will be happy with. If your bathroom gets too steamy, you may need to install an exhaust fan. This is the time to get to the root cause of your bathroom disorganization. It may be that you have the organizing tools, but no one uses them. In that case, you need to establish a better clean-up routine for your whole family to adopt.

What's in your bathroom now? Pull everything out of the cabinets. Take things out of the tub or shower area and begin to categorize them. Then do the same thing to your linen closet. Write down all the categories on your room organizing sheet to see if there is anything that should not be in the bathroom area. Combine categories that are in both the bathroom and the linen closet.

What do you want to keep in the bathroom? Some essential bathroom items you'll want to keep are:

- Two rolls of toilet paper (one on the holder plus one extra)
- Toothbrushes and toothpaste (one or two tubes maximum)
- Hand soap
- Shampoo and conditioner
- Body wash or soap for the bath/shower
- Washcloths, a hand towel, and a bath towel for each person
- Cosmetics (if you put them on in the bathroom)
- Hair supplies (if you do your hair in the bathroom)
- Step stool or potty seat for small children
- Bath toys in a container (if they can't be kept in the linen closet)

Look at the piles of categories you have created and decide what can be tossed. Here are some obvious ones: moldy bathroom toys, towels that are thread bare, medicines that have expired, old toothbrushes, and bath mats that are shedding. Don't fret too much about getting rid of these items. Most of them are inexpensive and can easily be replaced.

Purge: If you find you have too much of one category, pare it down. Some categories that tend to accumulate in bathrooms and linen closets are: medicines, cosmetics, travel size lotions and shampoos, towels, bath toys, nail polishes, perfumed bath salts and beads that you receive as presents, and cleaning products.

If you are really tight for space in the linen closet, keep extra sheets in the bedroom closets.

Consider what you really need and use. If some sundries are still good, but you don't use them, try to find a shelter or nursing home to donate them to. Box up the donations and move them out of the bathroom along with the trash.

Rearrange: Look at what you will be keeping in your bathroom and where it will go. If you have cabinet space under the sink or in a medicine cabinet, begin to put your essential items in them. If you have a plastic bin with holes in it or a mesh bag for bath toys, it's okay to keep them in the bath because they are contained. If you've got too many bath toys to keep in one container, store some in another bin and keep it in the linen closet or under the sink. As you put everything back in, you will probably notice where you need containers or bins. If you are really tight for space in the linen closet, you could keep extra sheets in the bedroom closets or extra blankets in another area of the house. My grandmother taught me this trick for keeping a set of sheets together: Place the folded fitted and top sheets inside the pillowcase. Space bags, which allow you to store several comforters, blankets and sheets in a smaller container by vacuuming out the air, are also a great way to make room in a linen closet.

What needs to be added to this room? Jot down what types of organizers you need and then go shopping! Make sure you have the measurements of the cabinets or drawers to buy the right size. In the meantime you can store your bath items in boxes that are labeled with the category until you can transfer them into your new organizers. Whatever you want to change about the bathroom, write it down and price out what the changes will cost. Organize what you have before you take on any major remodeling. Like the kitchen, it's easier to see what improvements you need when a bathroom is cleared out. It will also be much easier to put things back in the bathroom when they are categorized and contained.

To keep a set of sheets together, place the folded fitted and top sheets inside the pillow case.

MAINTAINING YOUR BATHROOM

Once you have reorganized your bathroom, give your family a tour. Show the children where bathroom toys will be kept, and make sure everyone knows which towel set and toothbrush are theirs. If you have several people using one bathroom, it's a good idea to color code the towels. Demonstrate for your family how and where a wet towel is hung. Make it fun, but make sure everyone knows how to clean up after themselves. Let's face it, you're still going to

If you have several people using one bathroom, it's a good idea to color code the towels.

pick up after the little ones in the bathroom but maybe they can help you put the bath toys away. Ask the older children to hang up their towels and wipe off the counters and sink after they brush their teeth.

Before guests visit, I always check our main bath to make sure the toilet is flushed, there's toilet paper on the holder, towels are on the rack, the sink is toothpaste-free, and toys are in the bin. Then I light a candle and breathe a sigh of relief.

18. Everything Ends Up in the Family Room

THE PROBLEM

If you've only got one room to call the "family room," it can become quite cluttered. Most people use this room to watch television, which means that DVDs and videos are kept nearby. If your children are small, this may also be where toys, books, games and puzzles are kept. And if you have any social interaction, this is where guests gather when they visit.

Gone are the days of the formal "parlor" and the "children's nursery," when we could keep things separated. Now we have "great rooms" and "all-purpose" rooms. With so much happening there and so much stuff to store, these rooms can fill up fast.

THE STORY

I have a friend who has a small living room (about 13' × 16'; 4m × 5m). Her family of four uses this room to watch TV, read, play with toys and do the family paperwork. Because she is so organized, she has created zones and only keeps what she uses. As a result, her family room always appears cozy and not cluttered. Here is how she accomplishes it:

1. There are two tall bookcases that hold only the parent's books and framed photos.
2. There is a small desk where the mail goes to be sorted, and bills are paid.
3. There is a small TV on a table with storage underneath for videos.
4. There is a small shelf under the window that holds baskets of children's toys and puzzles.
5. The coffee table has a shelf underneath for children's games.
6. Bigger toys are kept in decorative floor baskets, and the remaining toys are stored in the basement.
7. The sofa and love seat are arranged in an "L" position along the walls, facing the TV and the big window, leaving an open area in the middle of the room.

Everything has a place in this room and there is adequate storage, which makes for easy clean up. It's a great example of making the best of a small living room.

THE SOLUTION

Recall the functions of your family room. Then use the Room Organizing Worksheet (page 187) to plan how you will organize your family room.

Remember to think positive and keep favorable aspects of the room intact.

What do you like about the room currently? Is it cozy? Is it wide open? Does it have a lot of natural light? Remember to think positive and keep those aspects of the room intact.

What don't you like about the room currently? Maybe the room doesn't have a lot of light. Maybe there's no style to the room because you've been adding furniture without an overall plan to decorate. Maybe there's too much going on in this room and it's cluttered. Whatever the case, decide what you want to change about the room as you organize.

What is in the room now? Make a list of the categories of items as well as the furniture. If objects are scattered all over the room, pile like things together so you can assess your situation. If you haven't already, pare down your possessions in this room. Refer back to the chapters in Part II of this book to organize things such as photos, memorabilia, paperwork and toys. Any of those items that do not belong should be boxed up and moved to the correct room.

Absolute of Organizing: Keep like things together.

What do you want to keep in this room? It should be the bare essentials of what you like and the things you need to make this room functional. This list will be your starting point for rearranging.

What, if anything, needs to be added to this room, and do you need to hire someone? If you know at this point that you would like a contractor to come in, continue to organize the room as best you can before you call for quotes or go shopping. If you don't know what needs to be added at this point, simply skip this question and come back to it after you have categorized, purged and rearranged.

> *The trickiest living rooms are those with two focal points, like a fireplace and a TV.*

Absolute of Organizing: Use the C.P.R. process: Categorize, Purge and Rearrange

PUTTING IT ALL TOGETHER

Once you are left with what stays in the family room, set up zones for different activities.

Two focal points. The trickiest living rooms are those with two focal points, like a fireplace and a TV. You want to have the seating facing the TV for obvious reasons, but it's also nice to have a conversation area where people can sit and enjoy the fire and actually talk to each other. To do this, you have a few options.

1. Put the TV along the same wall as the fireplace, combining your focal points.
2. Put the TV on the opposite wall and partition the room into two areas, one for sitting by the fire, and one for watching TV.
3. Put the TV on an adjacent wall to the fireplace and keep the furniture in an open angle where you could look at either one from the same sitting area.

Areas that flow. If you choose the third option above, you are creating areas that flow. Going along with this idea, you really don't need to divide your room in any way. If you like the idea of one big room for children to play, people to read or sit by a fire, and a place to watch television, then you can have a family room with a wide-open middle area and furniture along the walls. However, when it comes to storage, you still want to have zones. For instance, you can store your books and CDs along one wall, then have a box or basket for toys along another. If there are games and puzzles in this room, keep them all in one cabinet or on one shelf. This type of set up works well in a small area and is almost a necessity when you have limited space.

Distinctive zones. If you've got a large, square family room or one that is long and narrow, you may want to partition your room into distinctive areas. Some possible areas might be a recreation zone (for TV, music, and playing), a quiet reading area, or an office area. You can create these zones with area rugs by putting one in the middle of the recreation zone and one in the quiet reading area or the office zone. Or you can choose to leave one area without a rug. You can also partition with furniture by placing a chair or a sofa with its back to one area, and then set up everything behind that piece of furniture for a different purpose. If you have a studio apartment or a large basement

Use rugs or furniture to create distinctive areas within a large, open room.

Family Room

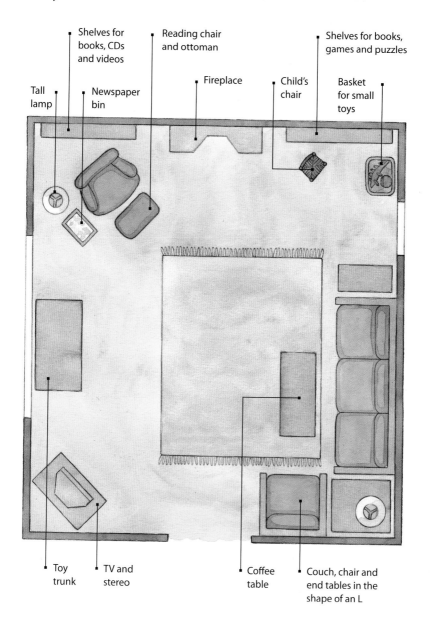

Shelves for books, CDs and videos

Reading chair and ottoman

Shelves for books, games and puzzles

Tall lamp

Newspaper bin

Fireplace

Child's chair

Basket for small toys

Toy trunk

TV and stereo

Coffee table

Couch, chair and end tables in the shape of an L

for your family room and you want to divide a room without putting up a wall, you can use standing screens, a large curtain or shelving units to create a more "movable" wall. Just remember the larger the room, the more zones you can have, but I still recommend only using each room for two to three functions. Any more than that and you will have a room that feels chopped up.

> *Even though your family room may be the place where everything happens in your home, you don't have to keep everything there.*

Hidden treasures. When space is at a premium in your house, you've got to start looking for hidden treasures. I mean little improvements or storage options that will have a big impact on the organization of a room. One hidden treasure that I found when we moved from our old house to our current one is built-in bookshelves and cabinets. We have one wall in the family room that has seven bookshelves, two small cabinets and four large cabinets that run the length of the wall. I am amazed at all the stuff this wall system holds! It holds our massive video and DVD collection, and eight storage bins of toys underneath. The two small cabinets hold all of our family's games and puzzles. I once considered built-ins a luxury item that I couldn't afford. But if you add up the shelving and storage bins you buy over time, investing that money in custom cabinets could be a simple solution to your family's storage issues. This type of storage is also flexible for families of all ages. I can envision our children's movies and toy bins being replaced with trophies and sports equipment as my children get older.

Other hidden treasures could be furniture with storage. Consider an ottoman in which you can store toys or blankets. Always opt for end tables and coffee tables with a drawer or a shelf underneath. Have a TV stand or entertainment center that will hold all of your electronic equipment and your CDs, DVDs and videos if possible. Decorative trunks or floor baskets are great places to store your family room items to keep it looking stylish.

Also remember that even though your family room may be the place where everything happens in your home, you don't have to keep everything there. Use storage options around your house and bring the toys or projects in and out as necessary.

19. I'm Living Out of My Minivan!

THE PROBLEM

You are a mom, and therefore a chauffeur as well. Some of us drive from day care to work and back again every day. Others drive to doctor's appointments, pre-school and the supermarket. In the afternoon, we drive to ballet, music lessons and soccer. We also know children do not travel light, especially when they are young. There are diaper bags, snacks, and sports equipment to remember. For safety reasons you want to have your car or minivan well equipped for anything that might happen during your travels. Inevitably someone is screaming for something you don't have as you set out for the day's errands and appointments.

THE STORY

A few years ago, I made the mistake of letting my husband pack our car for va-cation. We had only been on the road half an hour when my youngest asked for a drink. "The cooler is in the back," my husband said. So I had to instruct my daughter how to climb in the back of the station wagon, move a few items and dig out a drink. Not only was this unsafe, but it was messy. When the next child asked for a snack, I told him to look in the grocery bag by his feet, but unfortunately there were only canned goods, bread and cereal in the sack. I knew instinctively what the children would want during our two-hour drive, but my husband figured if the children wanted something, they could either wait until we got there or they would bring it themselves. He was just happy that we got everything in one car! From then on, my husband has let me pack the car for any long trips, and I have fine-tuned the art of strategically packing a car for three children.

THE SOLUTION

Be prepared and have your car packed with essentials for both you and your children. Look at the items listed below and then take a notebook with you as you drive around for a week. Write down anything the children ask for that you don't have, as well as anything you wish you had. This will become your personal wish list for your car.

Safety Items

- Gas container and funnel
- Jumper cables
- Cell phone charger for car
- Fix-a-flat
- Spare tire and jack
- Road flares
- Cell phone
- Ice scraper
- Maintenance book for your car

Convenience Items

- Deposit slips for the bank—make it easier to use the drive-thru
- Maps of places you travel to often
- Directions and phone numbers of out-of-town friends you visit
- Baby wipes—great for spills on clothing, seats and console areas
- Loose change—if you need to pay tolls
- A snack, gum or mints
- A change of clothes or coveralls—in case you have to change a flat tire
- Sun shield for the side windows and the windshield
- Pen and paper

Baby Needs

- Pacifier
- Diapers and wipes
- Change of clothes
- Teething gel
- Little toys
- Little blanket
- Baby food or bottle
- Acetaminophen or ibuprofen

Toddler Needs

- Snacks
- Little toys
- Diapers
- Books
- Change of clothes
- Baby wipes
- A towel—to wipe off playground equipment after it rains

Grade Schooler's Needs

- Drink or snack
- Hand-held toy
- Book
- A big blanket

Teenager's Needs

- Portable music player
- Book

Absolute of Organizing: Start with a good list.

PUTTING IT ALL TOGETHER

Now that you have a list of everything you want to keep in your car, start to assemble these items. Categorize them according to where they need to be in the car. Your items should be kept up front. Items the children need should be within reach in the second seat. Any safety items can be stored in the trunk or back of the car. Find appropriate containers for each area such as the glove compartment or side door pockets in the front seat, a back-of-the-seat organizer for the children's things, or a small diaper bag to leave in the car for the baby. The tools and car care equipment can fit in a tool box or a plastic milk crate in the trunk or back of the car.

Road trips. When taking car trips that are two hours or longer, we pack the portable TV in between the two front seats and let the children watch a movie. I also make sure that everyone is as comfortable as possible, with shoes off, pillows and blankets and everything they could ask for within reach, before we leave our driveway! Before a long trip, I also visit the dollar store to buy inexpensive toys for the children. Each hour I'll hand out something new to keep them occupied.

Everyday errands. For short jaunts to the store or school, put the child who needs to be buckled in right behind the driver's seat. Older children who can buckle themselves can go on the other side of the back seat. This will save you from having to run around your car or climb in the back of your minivan every time you go out.

Your purse and diaper bag. If you don't want to feel bogged down with baggage every time you leave the house, consolidate your purse and the baby's diaper bag. First, take a look at what you bring with you for every trip in the car. See if you have one bag that can accommodate all those things, and leave it by the door. I love to use backpacks of all sizes because they allow your hands to be free to carry a baby or to hold a child's hand when crossing a parking lot. If you use a basic backpack instead of a standard "diaper bag," even Dad won't mind carrying it. If there's anything you can leave in the car, pack a small bag and leave it there. These items might include a baby's change of clothes, spit up pads, diapers and wipes, a pacifier, some snacks for the children, and little toys. For yourself, you may like to have tissues, a small makeup case, a brush and some gum or mints. If these items are always in the car, then all you have to grab when you leave is your wallet, keys and cell phone. Several women I know often leave their entire handbag in the car. No matter where you live or how safe you think your car is, *this is a bad idea!* It's too easy for keys to get locked in or for your wallet to be stolen. Instead, consolidate your daily travel items, chose a nice, easy bag to carry and either leave it in the car without your valuables, or leave it by the door in your home.

Absolutely Organized

Congratulations! If you followed every chapter in this section, you should now have a completely organized home. At the very least, you should have a plan to attain that goal.

REMEMBER

- Create a Home Projects Plan that gives you a vision of what you want to do in each room of your house.
- Work on one room at a time.
- Use the "Room Organizing Worksheet" (page 187) to plan how you will organize each room.
- Decide the functions of each room first.
- A home office can be as simple as a desk and file cabinet.
- Plan what needs to be stored in your home and what purpose each storage area will serve.
- Kitchen or bathroom counters should hold only what you use every day.
- An organized refrigerator is a healthy one.
- Limit your children's toys, knickknacks and artwork with practically sized containers.
- Maximize your closet space so more items can be put away.
- Designate zones for different functions in your family room.
- Equip your vehicle with everything you need to travel with kids.
- Teach your family how to maintain the beautifully organized home you have created!

Appendices

ABSOLUTES OF ORGANIZING

1. C.P.R. is the method: Categorize, Purge and Rearrange.
2. Keep purging simple with "Yes" and "No" piles.
3. Keep only what you use.
4. If you don't plan it, it won't happen.
5. Keep like things together.
6. Start with a good list.
7. Subtract before you add.
8. Finish one thing before you start another.
9. Organize from large to small.
10. Daily routines are a must.

WHAT EVERY MOM NEEDS

There are certain organizational items that I believe no mom or family should be without. You may have some of these already, but you really need all of them to run your family efficiently.

1. Daily planner
2. Family calendar
3. Stair basket
4. House Projects Plan book
5. Home office
6. Notebook—kept where you do your best thinking
7. Coupon caddy
8. Perpetual food list
9. Folder for children's activities and school information
10. A memory box for each family member

DEBBIE LILLARD'S ROOM ORGANIZING WORKSHEET

Room: _____

Function of room
1. _____
2. _____
3. _____

What do you like about the room currently? _____
_____

What don't you like about the room currently? _____
_____

What is in the room now? (List categories of items)
_____   _____
_____   _____

What do you want to keep in this room?
_____   _____
_____   _____

What if anything needs to be added to the room? _____
_____

What contractors do you need to hire? _____
_____

If needed, get three labor/materials estimates:
1. _____
2. _____
3. _____

Index